Sport and Work

European Perspectives
A Series of the Columbia University Press

SPORT
AND
WORK

Bero Rigauer

Translated by Allen Guttmann

New York
COLUMBIA UNIVERSITY PRESS
1981

Bero Rigauer is Professor of Sociology at the University of Oldenburg, Federal Republic of Germany.

Allen Guttmann is Professor of American Studies at Amherst College

Library of Congress Cataloging in Publication Data

Rigauer, Bero, 1934–
  Sport and work.

  (European perspectives)
  Translation of: Sport und Arbeit.
  Includes bibliographical references and index.
  1. Sports—Philosophy. 2. Sports—Social aspects.
  3. Work—Social aspects. 4. Behaviorism (Psychology)
  5. Sports—Psychological aspects. 6. Work—Psychological aspects. I. Title. II. Series.
  GV706.R4713   796'.01   81-793
  ISBN 0–231–05200–6   AACR2

Columbia University Press
New York   Guildford, Surrey

Copyright © 1981 by Columbia University Press

Sport und Arbeit © 1969, 1979 by Bero Rigauer.
First Published by Suhrkamp Verlag, Frankfurt.

Contents

Translator's
Introduction

Playful movement is a human universal. All children and most adults have moments of frolic and gambol. The infant Hercules wrestled; Krishna danced; the Norse gods played with the weapons of war. This playful movement, indulged in for no other apparent purpose than the pleasure of the activity, is a phenomenon shared with the animal kingdom. "Play," wrote the great Dutch historian Johan Huizinga, "is older than culture, for culture, however inadequately defined, always presupposes human society, and animals have not waited for man to teach them how to play."[1] While biologists and psychologists are interested in those aspects of play shared by men and animals, historians from the time of Herodotus have concerned themselves with play as an element of culture. As early as 1801, the English historian Joseph Strutt noted the great advantage of playful activity as an index to cultural differences:[2]

> In order to form a just estimation of the character of any particular people, it is absolutely necessary to investigate the Sports and Pastimes most generally prevalent among them. War, policy [politics], and other contingent circumstances, may effectually place men, at different times, in different points of view, but, when we follow them into their retirements,

where no disguise is necessary, we are most likely to see them in their true state, and may best judge of their natural dispositions.

It is precisely the activity which is least consciously a manifestation of culture that tells us most about the inevitable cultural differences dividing up the family of man.

Since frolic and gambol and spontaneous play in general seem indeed to be human universals, historians have seldom paused to remind us that *Homo sapiens* has always had moments of whirling about and leaping up and down. It is when play becomes characterized by rules, when it turns into a game, that historians—at least some of them—become interested. When the game takes the form of a contest, which not all games do, when the contest is one of physical prowess, which is what sports are all about, sociologists take notice. Frolic has become football. In modern society, playful movement has become an institutionalized activity involving millions of people as participants and hundreds of millions as spectators. The result is that sociological analysis of the Olympic Games or of the National Basketball Association has become almost as respectable as the study of class structure in a factory town or social role in a hospital. The sociology of sports is here to stay.

German scholarship can claim credit for the first monograph devoted to the sociology of sports, Heinz Risse's brilliant little book, *Soziologie des Sports* (1921), which drew upon the work of Karl Marx, Ferdinand Toennies, and Max Weber in order to argue for the unique role of sports in industrial-capitalist society. Although sports have incorporated a "positivistic" aspect of modern society—i.e., regular training, quantified measurement of achievement, and the quest for records—they nonetheless provide a "reaction against the entire system within which man is reduced to a machine."[3] For Risse, sports provide an area of Nietzschean achievement apart from the routine drabness of bourgeois society. "Only in the realm of physical culture [i.e., sports] can the mechanized man of today express his will [to be an individual]."[4] Only in sports can modern man overcome the barriers of class and reach the egalitarian ends of socialism.

A little less than fifty years after the publication of *Soziologie des Sports* Bero Rigauer's brilliant little book, *Sport und Arbeit* (1969), drew upon the Marxist tradition in order to characterize modern sports not as the heroic alternative to industrial-capitalist society but rather as its mirror image. Although Rigauer did not set out systematically to refute Risse's thesis (Rigauer's shots are fired after other *bêtes noirs*), it is uncanny how completely his book contradicts the earlier classic. *Sport und Arbeit* is the Neo-Marxist reply to the Nietzschean attempt to establish the athlete as the modern hero.

One must insist upon the term "Neo-Marxist" even if it complicates what might have been a simple dichotomy between Marxist and non-Marxist approaches. Although Rigauer depends far less on psychoanalytic theory than do other Neo-Marxists who have joined him in the critique of modern sports, his work cannot be characterized simply as "Marxist."

Since Marxists and Neo-Marxists have wholly incompatible interpretations of modern sports, it is necessary to insist upon the distinction between them. Since the distinction is not always a familiar one to American readers, a summary view of it is in order.

The Neo-Marxists have attempted to combine the insights of Marx with those of Freud. Leaving aside the question of whether or not such a combination is logically possible, we can certainly point to a distinguished and influential group of thinkers who made the attempt. For a number of years, the *Frankfurter Institut für Sozialforschung* (Frankfurt Institute for Social Research) brought together such men as Theodor Adorno, Erich Fromm, Max Horkheimer, and Herbert Marcuse, all of whom have had a significant impact on American as well as European social thought. Although the seizure of power by the Nazis in January 1933 spelled the end for the Frankfurt Institute as such, most of its members escaped to the United States, where their criticism of "mass society" continues to condition the way we understand and react to our social order.

What was their criticism? How did they seek to combine Marx and Freud? Simplified greatly, their argument was that industrial capitalism was exactly what Marx had called it—a system of economic exploitation of workers by capitalists. What Marx had not fully reckoned with was the tenacity of the system. He had assumed that the working class, with the help of the Communist Party, would develop its class consciousness to the point where the injustices of capitalism seemed too much to be borne, at which point the proletariat would break its economic chains and rise in revolt. Unfortunately, Marx underestimated the possibilities of psychological manipulation. Enter Freud. The Neo-Marxists of the Frankfurt Institute saw in Freud's psychoanalytic theories, especially in his discovery of the unconscious mind, the key to the mystery of capitalism's unexpected longevity. Intellectuals acting in the interest of the ruling class have created a "false consciousness" in the proletariat. The worker imagines that his good is identical with that of his employer. In specific terms, the automobile worker casts his ballot for Dwight David Eisenhower, the bank clerk votes for Richard Milhous Nixon.

Freudian theory was used not only to explain the passivity of the worker in the fact of exploitation but also to account for his eagerness to work and for the sexual repression which allegedly characterizes the United States. In Herbert Marcuse's analysis, repressed sexual energies are economically useful to the capitalist in that they can be released in the form of work. There is, in other words, a necessary relationship between Victorian sexual inhibition and industrial capitalism.

From their Marxist-Freudian social theory, Adorno, Marcuse, and their younger Neo-Marxist followers have drawn very negative conclusions about modern sports, but these negative conclusions are most definitely *not* shared by most Marxists. While Marxist scholars in various countries have emphatically criticized the commercialism and the racism as well as the alleged nationalism, imperialism, and militarism of American and Western European sports, they have with equal or greater emphasis praised the role of sports in the Soviet Union and in the other nations of the Warsaw Pact. Marxist scholars like the Polish sociologist Andrzej Wohl have written eloquently on bourgeois sports as an instrument of repression, but they have gone on to speak enthusiastically about sports in their own countries as a means to bring about the birth of what they commonly refer to as "new socialist man."[5] In the Marxist view, the sports officially encouraged by the Communist Party are a necessary part of a humanistic world view. They are also a way of increasing economic productivity, of providing for military defense, and of demonstrating the superiority of Communism in international athletic encounters.[6] It is precisely this love-is-blind, pro-sports ardor of Marxist scholarship which makes it essential to identify the radical criticism of sports as Neo-Marxist.

This radical criticism first appeared in systematic form in Bero Rigauer's *Sport und Arbeit* and made that book the landmark it has since become. While sports have always had their critics, from Euripides to Harry Edwards and Jack Scott, it was *Sport und Arbeit* which most effectively called into question not the abuses but the very essence of sports, not the violations of the rules but the rules themselves. It was *Sport und Arbeit* which questioned the idealized version of sports enshrined in a thousand boys' books and a thousand after-dinner orations. Rigauer's criticism, moreover, was not based on that instinctive dislike of physical activity which has traditionally characterized a number of intellectuals but rather on a belief in the importance of play. What is truly radical about Rigauer's book is his argument that sports are not a playful alternative to the world of work but rather its mirror image. Sports are, in the words of another young Neo-Marxist, "the capitalistically distorted form of play."[7]

If the American reader's initial response to such criticism is puzzlement, the reason lies partly in our national tendency toward a "pragmatic" suspicion of social theory and partly in the fundamental nature of Rigauer's perceptions. His critique of sports is so radical that readers accustomed to the "radicalism" of a protest against racism in sports find it difficult to understand exactly what Rigauer has done. Quite simply, he has gone to the root of the matter.

Rigauer begins with the traditional "bourgeois" interpretation of the relation between sports and work. He cites Carl Diem (1882–1962), the great German sports administrator and scholar, who saw sports and work as polar opposites. On the contrary, answers Rigauer; sports and work are structurally analogous. Both are characterized by what the American psychologist David McClelland, building on the work of Henry Murray, called "the achievement principle," the tendency to strive competitively for some kind of socially recognized excellence. "Individual achievement, not inherited symbols of status, functions as the criteria for social mobility."[8] As the doctor rises by his mastery of medical techniques, as the lawyer wins status by his forensic skill, as the physicist and chemist are esteemed for their contributions to scientific knowledge, so does the athlete demonstrate his physical prowess. Status ascribed on the basis of race, religion, class, or sex is irrelevant. Although the achievement principle characterizes sports at all levels from sandlot softball to the Olympic Games, top-level sports show the most striking congruity with work, where achievement has for generations been accepted as the prerequisite for success.

In order for social status to be allocated on the basis of achievement, we need rationalized standards against which achievements can be objectively measured. It is, therefore, no accident that our modern sports are subjected to the same kinds of measurements as our modern work. "Athletic achievements now take place in the 'objective framework' of the 'c-g-s' (centimeter, gram, second) system and in point scores which rely either upon objectively measurable achievements (as in the pentathlon and decathlon) or in subjective judgments (as in team games, gymnastics, boxing, etc.)."[9] As workers and athletes increasingly adapt themselves to mechanical requirements, machines become increasingly important both at work and in sports, where technological advance plays a role both in the improvement of traditional sports implements, like the fiberglass pole for the pole vault, and in the invention of wholly new technological sports, like automobile, motorboat, and airplane races.

Part and parcel of this desire to turn every social action into a quantified achievement of machine-like precision is the "scientification" of both work and sports. *Everything* is studied with an eye to its rationalization and control, and sports are certainly no exception. Physiologists study oxygen intake and the ability of the blood to carry off accumulations of lactic acid; psychologists study the U-curve of anxiety in order to determine optimal levels of pre-game nervous tension; sociologists study the socialization of children into sports in order to facilitate the process and thus maximize the pool of potential champions.

Once we set up objective standards as our criteria for achievement, it is all but inevitable that we begin to train, i.e., rationally, systematically, scientifically to prepare ourselves for the necessary level of achievement. This, argues Rigauer, is as true of sports as of the world of work. The athlete who trains for five or ten years with an Olympic medal in mind is not fundamentally different from the man or woman who studies economics for five or ten years in order to earn the academic degrees certifying scholastic achievement and qualifying for professional advancement. Sport, like work, becomes increasingly specialized. This is especially evident in training, where, as Rigauer points out, the athlete spends more time than in actually competing. In training we see the extremes of rationalization characteristic of the theories of the American "social engineer" Frederick W. Taylor. It was Taylor of course who introduced the notion of a systematic study of human motion in order to discover the most efficient and economical way of performing any given physical task. Taylor employed paper and pencil whereas the contemporary sport physiologist employs a computer, but the principle is the same: how can one achieve a maximum effort with a minimum expenditure of energy? What physical motion is the most economical? It is Rigauer's contention that this kind of approach leads inevitably to the dismemberment of the action. One learns separate motions or, in team games, tactics and "plays." One imitates the mechanical perfection of the physiologists's mathematical formulae. Small wonder that training has become repetitive, tedious, and, in a word, "mechanical."

The next step is bureaucratization. "Rationalization assumes logically necessary forms when it goes on to become bureaucratization and administration of top-level sports."[10] It is all but impossible to imagine a society characterized by the achievement principle which is not at the same time a bureaucratically organized society, because bureaucratic organization is by definition (if not always in practice) a hierarchy determined on the basis of achievement. Traditional hierarchy depends upon ascribed status; princes rule paupers because of the accidents of birth; the Brahmin caste performs priestly functions because priestly functions are ascribed to the Brahmin caste. But the rationalization of modern society implies hierarchy on the basis of function and function implies some kind of achievement. Bank presidents boss bank tellers because they presumably know more about banking and not because their fathers were bank presidents. (That we are indignant to find out that their fathers *were* bank presidents is simply another sign that we have internalized the achievement principle and see injustice in its violation.) Bureaucracy in sports and in work means goals, purposeful activity, planning, a system of social roles and ordered status. Bureaucracy "constantly narrows the individual's room for choice."[11]

At this point in his analysis, Rigauer turns to the specifically Marxist conception of labor as a commodity. "The athlete's achievement is transformed into a commodity and is exchanged on the market for its equivalent value, expressed in money."[12] It is not simply a question of "amateur" versus "professional" status because that distinction, dear as it may be to the idealists of the International Olympic Committee, no longer discriminates between those who practice sports as an avocation and those for whom sports are a way of life. Olympic amateurs may not receive a regular salary from swimming or skiing, but they obviously have exchanged athletic ability for the means of subsistence. In Marxist terms, for the means to "reproduction."

Given the nature of the capitalist system, it is not surprising that amateur athletes usually sell themselves cheaply—the material advantages (food, clothing, tuition, travel, etc.) can be considerable, but the profits reaped by the organizers (universities, clubs, National Olympic Committees, etc.) are often even greater. Although professional athletes are paid openly by owners who admit their ownership, the structure of relationships is really no different from that in amateur sports. The reduction of human personality to commodity, which is allegedly typical of capitalist society in general, reaches its point of absurdity in sports where one speaks of a "9.9-second-man" in the 100-meter dash or a "$1,000,000 pitcher" in baseball. "Behind these quantifications, the living human, with his special qualities, disappears."[13] In other words the dehumanization intrinsic to this kind of quantification is abetted if not actually caused by the market relations of modern industrial capitalism. Human achievements are reduced to abstract forms *because* one needs to sell them as commodities in the marketplace.

Although it is not essential to the logic of his argument, Rigauer also discusses the frequency of shared language in work and in sports. One speaks of a "good workout" or of "weight-work." One thinks in terms of "technique," i.e., mean to ends. "The sociological context is obvious: *Homo ludens* [man the player] remains *Homo faber* [man the maker], even in top-level sports."[14] At this point in his argument, Rigauer pauses to summarize: "Our preliminary thesis is, therefore, that top-level sports (but not sport in general) integrates work-like schemes of behavior and intellectual content into its system of behavior. Sports function as a sector of social conformity to industrial, bureaucratic social relationships."[15]

The apparent distinction between top-level sports and what one might call recreational sports is quickly erased when Rigauer goes on to remark, "Every assertion about the phenomenon of top-level sports is relevant for sports in general."[16]

Rigauer turns in part II, "Sport and Ideology,"

to the reasons behind the congruity of sports and work. Once again, Carl Diem represents "bourgeois" sports with his assertion that sports are "an emergence out of the great realm of life which is play."[17] Why have Diem and others been determined to trace a line of separation between sports and work? Why does the "official" theory of sports deny that sports and work are structurally identical? The reason is the desire to preserve the ideology of sports, to continue to use this ideology "to cement existing social relationships."[18] By harping on the Latin tag from Juvenal's *Satires, mens sana in corpore sano* [a sound mind in a sound body], bourgeois ideologues have made physical education into a means of political indoctrination. The language of German physical educators, like that of American coaches, is saturated with political suggestiveness. "Concepts like drive, conscientiousness, recognition of authority and of the achievements of one's superiors, modesty and shyness, the good of the group, etc., encourage conformity to the existing system of action and control."[19] In the 1930s, bourgeois exploitation became Nazi terror and the "sound body" of the bourgeois theorists became the hardened "Aryan" body of Nazi ideology. Belief in the physical superiority of the "Aryan" became a part of Adolf Hitler's racism, and it was only a step to the notion that the "pure blood" of the "Aryan" should be protected at all costs from defilement by "Semitic blood." The most complete protection from pollution involved the elimination of the very possibility of defilement, i.e., the extermination of the Jews. It is Rigauer's contention that Hitler's views of sports were an integral aspect of Nazism.

Rigauer ends not with this reminder of the ideological uses of sports but with a brief conclusion, "Toward a New Understanding of Sports," which calls for change. Once we are fully aware of the essential identity of sports and work and of the ideological purposes served by denying this identity, we can be free to effect changes, to democratize sports, to return, at least to some degree, to the marvelous spontaneity of frolic and gambol. But this kind of change, warns Rigauer, is possible only when the entire society is changed. Since sports always mirror social structure, humane sports will be possible only in a truly humane society.

Sport und Arbeit was but the first, although perhaps the best, of a whole wave of Neo-Marxist books and articles critical of American, French, and (West-) German sports.[20] These works share a common interpretation of the rise of modern sports, which they see as essentially the product of capitalism. They agree with Rigauer, and with a considerable number of non-Marxist authors, in their analysis of the achievement principle and the resultant rationalization, specialization, bureaucratization, quantification, and obsession with records of modern sports.

Many of the Neo-Marxists who have entered the ideological lists since the publication of *Sport und Arbeit* go considerably further than Rigauer in the utilization of psychoanalytic concepts. In their arguments, they tend to follow Adorno and Maruse, who asserted the necessity of sexual repression within capitalist society. The argument is that repressed energies blocked from direct expression in the *Lustprinzip* (pleasure principle) find their outlet through the *Leistungssprinzip* (achievement principle), that is, in work. Sexual sublimation is in the interest of the ruling class. The system, however, does not function perfectly and there remains a certain amount of unused sexual energy which, if not drained off somehow, poses a threat to the political and economic system. Sports are therefore designed as a form of sublimation which releases the repressed sexual impulses unutilized in work. The energies are released in the form of physical aggression. In short, "the aggression derived from sexual repression can thus be released (*kompensiert*) through athletic achievements and competitions."[21] Unfortunately, the transformation of sublimated sexual energies into physical aggression is imperfect. Sexuality emerges in sports as sexuality, but it appears in the perverted forms of sadism, masochism, narcissism, and homosexuality: "The erotic life of the athlete demonstrates a strange schizophrenia; in its physiological aspects, it is heterosexual, but in its psychic aspects it corresponds to the erotic dispositions of early childhood, and it is accordingly homosexual."[22]

The psychic processes which control the athlete act also, through the psychological mechanism of identification, upon the spectator as well. The result is that the mass of spectators is rendered "apathetic, manipulated, fragmented,"[23] infantilized—in a word, dehumanized. For them as well as for the athletes, Eros has become Thanatos.

Thus the indictment. Needless to say, the Neo-Marxist critique of modern sports has not gone unanswered by "bourgeois" scholars.[24] A brief summary of their arguments is in order.

The first objection is that the characteristics of modern sports do not occur only in those societies whose economic order is capitalist. Marxist societies are also enthusiastically dedicated to the achievement principle. In fact, Marxist scholars pride themselves on their commitment to the achievement principle.[25] There is, ironically, far more skepticism about the achievement principle in the West than in the East. Similarly, the sports of the Soviet Union and the German Democratic Republic are as thoroughly rationalized, specialized, bureaucratized, quantified, and record-obsessed as are the sports of the United States or the Federal Republic of Germany.* The fantastic Olympic performances of the East-German team, representing a population of 16 million people, is unimaginable except on the basis of exactly the kind of "capitalist" sports system described by Rigauer in *Sport und Arbeit*. And that is exactly the kind of sports system the East Germans have constructed. Unlike the enterprising British tourist who won the first Olympic title in tennis in

---

* To this list of five characteristics, not necessarily adduced by any single Neo-Marxist as *the* five, I have added secularism and equality (in the sense of equal access to and equal treatment within the competition). See *From Ritual to Record*, pp. 15–55.

1896, the Olympic champions of East Berlin, Dresden, and Leipzig did not decide on the spur of the moment to drop their daily routines and have a go at sports. In the only reasonable sense of the term, they are professionals. This comment upon the pervasiveness of the characteristics of modern sports does not, however, pose a serious objection to Rigauer's work. It is, in fact, a form of agreement. Since all but the most doctrinaire Neo-Marxists admit that the Communist bloc exhibits many of the same undemocratic traits as the "capitalist" world, they can readily concede that the sports of the Soviet Union, East Germany, Cuba, and the other nations of the Communist world are almost as repressive and inhumane as the sports of Western nations.

The more serious debate is not over the existence of the structural characteristics in question but over the proposition that these characteristics are sufficient for us to decide that sports and work are structurally identical. Has Rigauer demonstrated that sports are but the mirror of work? Do sports distort and pervert spontaneous play? Do they dehumanize? It is at this juncture that non-Marxists and Marxists travel off together in one direction while the Neo-Marxists, shaking their heads at an unholy alliance, go in another.

What shall we say about the indictment? The first thing that needs to be said is that Rigauer's list of similarities in the structures of sports and work is insufficient to support the conclusions that sports and work are structurally identical and that they are almost equally repressive. Difficult as it is to arrive at any kind of objective knowledge about human motivation, we nonetheless cannot evade the problem of conscious choice. We must take seriously the notion that sports are a subcategory of the world of play and that, as such, they are ends in themselves. In other words, the consciousness of the actor is decisive. The athlete's motivation is crucial. Raking leaves is work and playing tennis is not because most of us distinguish between the two activities on the basis of motive and not on the basis of energy expended. We can easily imagine a reversal in motivation; leaf-rakers can rake for the fun of it and tennis-players can work grimly at a physical-education requirement. Michel Bouet and other scholars have applied the most sophisticated psychological techniques to the question of motivation. Using interviews, projective tests, personality inventories, and other devices from the toolshop of modern psychology, they have concluded that the athletes can be trusted when they insist, as most of them do, that their participation in top-level sports is a form of play, an assertion of their human freedom to do what they choose, an experience of self-actualization quite unlike the routine experience of work.[26] Rationalization, specialization, quantification, and the quest for records are seen not as "dehumanizing" but as enabling factors that encourage athletes to extend the boundaries of the humanly possible.

Athletes are inclined to agree with Rigauer that training is frequently mechanical, arduous, and tedious; it certainly resembles work more than the actual contest does. But it is nonetheless a distortion to emphasize training, as Rigauer does, and to forget the exhilaration of the skilled contest which training has made possible. Athletes are also likely to agree with Rigauer that bureaucratic organization is irksome. Indeed, administrative squabbles like those between the Amateur Athletic Union (AAU) and the National Collegiate Athletic Association (NCAA) can actually prevent contests in which the athletes themselves ardently desire to compete. On this point, however, athletes are likely to display the all-too-human tendency to take the benefits of bureaucratic organization for granted and to respond to its malfunctions with passionate dissatisfaction.

The Neo-Marxist counterargument is that the athletes' voices of affirmation are simply proof of the pervasiveness of "false consciousness" among the victims of the repressive system: "The athlete who labors under the illusion that he is exempted [from the system of repression] reveals himself *ipso facto* as the unwitting victim of sports socialization."[27] In other words, witness against the indictment is proof of guilt. Although Hans Lenk has shown in painstaking detail that the assertions about the alienation and manipulation of top-level athletes are logically untenable, there is ultimately no way to refute the Neo-Marxist argument that evidence contrary to the Neo-Marxist critique is the tainted product of "false consciousness."[28]

The debate about sports and sexual perversion is similarly frustrating. To the empirical evidence demonstrating that athletes are, for instance, homosexual no more often than the rest of the population,

Gerhard Vinnai can answer that the athlete's wife may satisfy him in some physiological sense, but the athlete's team-mates are the true objects of his erotic attachment.[29] In other words, conscious sexual behavior is no clue to unconscious sexual preference. The manifest choice of a heterosexual relationship is merely "cosmetic" and the latent homosexuality is "essential." Believers in Vinnai's type of analysis will believe and the rest of us will remain infidels. It is to Rigauer's credit that he is very reluctant to indulge himself in arguments as flimsy as Vinnai's.

There is, fortunately, another aspect of the psychological debate which is more amenable to empirical determination than the question of motivation and the problem of sexual perversion. The entire Neo-Marxist case for the psychological function of sports within the capitalist world depends upon the notion that there is a catharsis by which the frustrated and aggressive spectator can be purged of the hostility which threatens to destabilize the political and economic order. If catharsis does not occur, then sports cannot be said to render the spectators apathetic. But the empirical evidence, almost without exception, indicates that the catharsis theory—at least as it applies to sports—is invalid. Laboratory tests of the propensity to aggression show that subjects who have watched sports films are more aggressive than subjects who have watched other kinds of films; projective techniques utilized at the scene of sports events indicate that attendance at such events raises rather than lowers the level of aggressiveness of the spectators; the observations of "participant-observers" watching out for instances of violence accompanying or following athletic events make plain the association between spectatorship and the possibility of "hooliganism."[30] In short, a variety of indicators tends rather unambiguously to disconfirm the catharsis theory. Various investigations have shown, on the contrary, that attendance at sports events or simply watching filmed or televised games is likely to increase rather than decrease hostility and aggressiveness. In other words, any ruling class which relied upon sports to pacify its unruly and rebellious working class would be acting contrary to its own best interests.

There is another aspect of the debate which is amenable to empirical tests. Neo-Marxist analysis asserts that modern sports have a specific function which "bourgeois" scholars have characteristically sought to conceal and disguise. Sports serve as a means of socialization as well as a form of catharsis. Sports teach the worker to play by the "rules of the game" and to accept these arbitrary rules as part of the structure of social reality—i.e., unquestioningly. In addition, sports serve as a form of compensation. They provide an arena where the exploited and frustrated worker can feel a sense of personal achievement long since vanished from his life on the job. (That the worker has merely substituted one form of repression for another by submitting himself to the mirror image of the world of work is beside the point now as long as he has the illusion that he is free; it is the illusion which the capitalist allegedly wishes to promote.) Finally, as a kind of bonus for the capitalist, participation in sports improves the workers' health, reduces days lost to sickness, and generally raises the level of labor power which can be exploited by the employer.

This entire argument, which concerns the function of sports vis-à-vis the participant rather than the spectator, is undermined by what one might refer to as the "phenomenon of accumulated advantage." In every modern society, liberal or socialist, capitalist or Communist, the advantaged citizen participates in sports (and in most other cultural activities as well) more often than does the disadvantaged. What this means in more specific sociological terms is that the rich participate more often than the poor, professionals and managers more often than blue-collar workers, the university-educated more often than the high-school or grade-school educated, men more often than women, and (not surprisingly) the healthy more than the sickly.[31] Since Rigauer is most familiar with West German society, this state of affairs can perhaps be best illustrated with data from a pair of studies of sports participation in West Germany. Table 1 demonstrates clearly that membership in sports clubs is skewed so that upper-middle-class Germans are far more likely than lower-class Germans to be members.[32]

The disproportionate participation of the socially advantaged grows more pronounced as one moves up the scale of achievement from casual, recreational sports to top-level sports. While the advantaged of society—Communist as well as capitalist—are more likely to participate in sports than are the

Table 1
Social Class and Sports Participation

	Sports-Club Members (%)	West German Population (%)
Lower Class	36.5	51.9
Lower Middle Class	53.0	38.6
Upper Middle Class	10.0	4.6
Non-Classifiable	0.5	4.9

disadvantaged, they are even more likely to be over-represented at the top. They are, for example, far more likely to be members of a picked national or Olympic team. This can be seen in Table 2. The table compares German athletes of the 1968 Olympic team to the

Table 2
Sociological Characteristics of Olympic Athletes (1968)

	Olympic Team (%)	West German Youth (%)
Education		
Grade School	29.5	65
Some High School	35.8	26
Finished High School	34.7	8
Mobility		
Upward	34.2	17.5
Downward	11.1	22.4
Religion		
Protestant	65	51.1
Catholic	31	44.1
Other	3	4.8

comparable age group in the nation as a whole. One can see immediately that top-level athletes are better educated, more upwardly mobile, and more Protestant than others in their age cohort.[33] (Although Catholics might deny that Protestants are religiously advantaged, cross-cultural studies agree that Protestants usually have higher social status than Catholics.)

There can be only one conclusion from the data gathered in these studies and in others carried out in almost every modern society: if sports are indeed, as the Neo-Marxist claims, a mechanism of repression victimizing their devotees, then the advantaged of the world have inexplicably shoved the disadvantaged aside in order themselves to become the victims. Before one accepts this unlikely worldwide conversion of the advantaged to altruism, one ought at least to consider an alternative explanation. Perhaps modern sports are not a means of repression after all but rather an opportunity for self-realization and freedom of action which the wealthy, educated male seeks for himself. On the whole, this seems to be the more plausible explanation. Rigauer's criticism of *one* empirical study on the basis of its alleged "methodological weakness" does not seriously reduce the plausibility of the alternative explanation.[34]

To have concluded this is to have accepted a great deal of Rigauer's analysis of the structural similarities of sports and work in the modern world but to have rejected his contention that sports function repressively. One can grant the existence of many structural similarities and still insist that sports, even top-level sports, are different from the world of work in that the athlete chooses to accept the rules. We are liberated rather than repressed by the discipline we have freely chosen.

There is an exhilaration and a joy and a self-realization in sports which cannot be written off as "false consciousness." The abuses of sports are many, but sports ought not be characterized solely on the basis of these abuses. Despite this less than perfect agreement with Rigauer and the other young scholars inspired by Adorno and Marcuse, one must admit that they have raised a host of new questions which older sociologists of sports tended either not to ask or to ask in less precise and fruitful ways. Even an unreconstructed non-Marxist can profit by the give-and-take of intellectual debate stimulated by *Sport und Arbeit*.

March 1981   Allen Guttmann
                                      Amherst College

A Note on the Translation

Sociological German does not translate easily into English. Its grammar allows the construction of complicated abstract nouns which can be translated only in the form of still more complicated phrases or clauses. The result, as readers of Karl Marx (in English translation) may have noticed, can be awkward. This difficulty is, of course, in addition to the difficulty of every translation: does one seek fidelity to the original or does one concentrate on idiomatic "naturalness" in one's own language? I have attempted to deal with the problems posed by Bero Rigauer's *Sport und Arbeit* by opting generally for fidelity to the German original. The result is that the language may seem slightly foreign; the ideas may seem rather unfamiliar, especially if the reader is not at home in the intellectual world of Marxism. If the reader takes Rigauer's argument seriously, the unfamiliarity may, in the end, turn out to be an asset, a signal that here is something new, something different, something unusual.

One specific term requires special comment. The German word *Leistung* is usually translated as "achievement" or, less often, "performance." Influenced by the American social psychologist David C.

McClelland, German sociologists have taken to describing modern society as an "achieving society" or "achievement-oriented society" (*Leistungsgesellschaft*). They also refer to "achievement sport" or "performance sport" (*Leistungssport*), which makes very little sense when translated directly into English. What is meant is sports at the national or international level. A good translation of the key term *Leistungssport* might be "highly competitive sport," but I have chosen to use "top-level sports." The *Leistungssportler* in Rigauer's sense is the Olympian and not the most fiercely competitive of bumblers.

A.G.

Sport and Work

Introduction

Sports are no autonomous system of behavior; they appear along with numerous other social developments whose origins lie in early-capitalist bourgeois society.[1] Although sports have constituted a specific realm of social behavior, they remain embedded in interdependent social processes which account for their fundamental characteristics—discipline, authority, competition, achievement, goal-oriented rationality, organization, and bureaucratization, to name but a few. In modern industrial society, certain techniques of productive work have become such dominant models of conduct that they impose their norms even upon so-called leisure-time activities.[2] Sports have not been able to escape this imposition of norms. The division of labor, mechanization, automation, bureaucratization—in short, the rationalization of the production of goods and services—influence consciousness and behavior even in those areas which seem independent of the world of industrial work. Increasingly, sports integrate rationalizing tendencies within their structure of behavior. The progressive objectification of work appears in sports as well and carries its organizational consequences for both the form and content of sports with it.

Granted, this hypothesis about the social context of sport and work has been disputed. Hans Linde has recently sought to test two sociological theorems about sports-related forms of behavior:[3] the first is Helmuth Plessner's thesis that sport can serve as compensation for the frustrations and aggression resulting from vocational failure; the second is Jürgen Habermas's thesis that leisure-time behavior is structured by the occupational sphere and demonstrates similar types of behavior. Linde believes that his empirical investigation has refuted both theorems. He concludes that sports activities cannot compensate for occupational failures or disappointments. Quite the contrary. He argues that the people most in need of compensation participate least in sport. In response to Habermas, Linde argues that a "dictate of work" no longer appears within the realm of leisure-time activities: the "relationship of work to personal life-style" is today "essentially more differentiated and freer" than in the days when castes or classes tended to restrict productive relationships.[4]

Linde's study is certainly an important contribution to the empirical investigation of the connection between sports and work. Nonetheless, the methodological weakness of his analysis is obvious. His empirical methods are inadequate to the task of unearthing the deeper sociological relationships between behavior in work and in sport. His data-gathering is sociogeographically too narrow; the statistical sample does not provide a representative model of the relevant population; the questionnaire he used is inadequate. In addition, empirically obtained results about sports are socially predetermined and cannot provide reliable information about sports. The work-like behavior patterns in leisure generally and in sports particularly are historically conditioned and can be identified as such. The very consciousness of the person whom the empiricist questions is determined by a system of social categories.

Our analysis begins with the assumption that an immediate confrontation with the object to be investigated is a precondition for directly understanding the problem and is, therefore, our first hypothesis.

Karl Popper sees the beginning of sociological research in (1) "problematical observations," which are expressed through preliminary anticipations and hypotheses, and in (2) theoretical systems that are then to be tested by empirical checks.[5] The forms in which sports appear are not perceived by us as pure data in the manner of the natural sciences but rather as socially and historically preformed, continually changing phenomena. By means of a qualitative, content-oriented analysis, these institutionalized conceptual schemes can be revealed and critically discussed.

Part I

Sports and Work

1. *Two Contrasting Interpretations of the Sports-Work Problem*

Two contradictory hypotheses dominate the literature dealing with the relationship between sports and the world of work:

i. Sports and Work are Oppositely Structured Systems of Behavior

For Carl Diem, sports are "a manifestation of the larger realm of play. Play is activity performed for its own sake, that is, in contrast to work, which is concerned with the endless struggle for physical survival."[1] According to Diem, professional sports are indeed work because the professional athlete earns his living through sports: "Professional sports are . . . not 'Sport' but rather its opposite, a job. Professional sports belong to the category of entertainment industry, with which it shares a good deal of discipline and training."[2] For Diem, "pure" sports are sharply distinguished from "daily labor," which was "once performed by the lower class."[3] Analogous arguments can be found throughout the literature on sports and physical education. Sports are equated with play and detached from the world of work and purpose. For example, "We understand sports as play and see in them a contrast to work; for that reason, athletic achievement is fundamentally unlike the achievements of the world of work even if athletic achievement must be 'worked for.'" "In our view, sports would lose their essence if torn out of the context of play and turned into pure work within the realm of purposeful behavior." "In play, man frees himself once again from the world of work, of coercion, of purpose, and revives the deeper reality of his being."[4] The official representative of West German sports, the German Sport Federation (*Deutscher Sport Bund*), accepts this definition when it asks that sports be "an alternative to the world of work," that "*Homo faber* [man the maker] not be allowed to replace *Homo ludens* [man the player]." This alternative must be defended "with tooth and nail" in order to preserve "the freedom of sports."[5]

ii. Sports and Work are Structurally Analogous Schemes of Behavior

"One sometimes hears the opinion that sports are a protest of mankind against the displacement from nature and natural conditions which are brought about by urbanization and industrialization. I doubt that one can speak so generally." Arnold Gehlen came to this conclusion because he perceived the "inner structural similarity between sports and vocational life." Sports remain "a visibly altered mirror image of the serious and of the vocational." For instance, ball games "preserve in altered form the rules, demands for discipline, and particular moral traits of collective work."[6] Max Horkheimer and Theodore Adorno also refer to the significance of collectivism in sport and to the resulting social possibility that men can be degraded to a "mere biological species." In their view, sports typically promote adaptation to the industrial system. "The oarsmen who are unable to speak with one another are trapped in the same tempo as the modern factory worker."[7]

Many critics of sport see planning as a work-like element: "Sports have long since become an aspect of the rationalization of labor." One sees the truth of this thesis in modern training methods, which duplicate the world of work, which turn the training cycle into a productive process.[8] The mechanization of labor is a striking development "which also transforms play and subjects it to mechanical conditions."[9]

Helmuth Plessner uses the example of "leisure-time consciousness" to illustrate the intrusion of the world of work into every aspect of life. One attempts in one's free time to construct the opposite of the world of work, "an alternative society, a social behavior which is like play, but the very playfulness becomes the basis for a new world of work. One stands between two worlds of work and has no choice but to go from one to the other, recovering from the burdens of one by exhausting oneself in the other."[10] The principle of specialization is an integral part of modern sports and is symptomatic of the problem. Specialization has gone so far that the top-level athlete now needs vacations—from sports.[11]

Disparaging voices are now heard even from the ranks of sports functionaries. They are most critical of the fact that contemporary sports now assume the "typical attributes of technocracy." Sports have all too assiduously aped industrial society and its achievement principle and have become, all things considered, much too serious. In order to work effectively against this tendency, sports need to make room once more for "the unplanned and the entirely spontaneous, for the joy of the moment, and . . . for true play."[12]

The division of Germany [into East Germany and West Germany] has necessary consequences for the scientific study of sports. The description of sports as purposeless play and as an "alternative to the world of work" is predominant among West German authors, but the theorists of East Germany are decisive in their rejection of this interpretation. They base their case on the theorems of Marxist sociology. As they say, the "process of the development of human movement is not only a biological but also a social occurrence which is ultimately an economic development determined by society's productive relationships.[13] Their term "physical culture" should be understood as "the totality of social measures and activities aimed at the physical perfection of mankind."[14] Physical culture is a "component of the whole culture" and depends upon the level of material and spiritual production." Sports cannot be an end in themselves because every social action is purposeful; sports are rather "a child of modern means of production" and "their necessary result."[15] Here we see unveiled the behavioral affinity between sports and work. Historically, sports derive from the forms and functions of work; it can be assumed that "the majority of the physical exercises that we know today once possessed a productive character and satisfied particular human needs. However, this productive character was lost in the course of the development of sports."[16] The other side of the coin is that sports facilitate techniques of movement which can be applied to the productive process.[17] West-German authors, of course, write off this line of argument with the usual negative stereotype that it is merely the product of Communist ideology.[18] They overlook the fact that they themselves represent an ideological position.

2. *The Necessity of Social Labor*

Man is helpless in a biological sense: he is without natural weapons, without the means of flight from danger, and with senses that are inferior to those of the "specialists" in the animal world. Man creates what we call culture, or "second nature," and must in this capacity survive as an "acting creature."[1] Since the world, "as we find it before us, can never satisfy our needs," we need "permanent institutions . . . simply to survive."[2] Work is, accordingly, purposeful, directed activity whose aim is to satisfy our needs. This activity is dialectical, including both production and reproduction, appearing as a self-creating or self-objectifying human act."[3] "Human labor, simply as a means of being, cannot be separated from being human—not even in the 'product' of such labor."[4]

It follows that social labor cannot be comprehended or determined in isolation from the concrete social situation in which it occurs. It occurs under various economic conditions with the help of different technical-rational means and in the context of differing social forms with different kinds of political authority. Sociologists who study work define job-related human activities as kinds of behavior directed toward goals, toward success. "The goal of work can be the product of the activity itself or some other success attached to the product of the activity, e.g., a wage."[5] The crucial factor is human activity. Man is reduced to a measurable productive force. Within the context of this interpretation of human activity the connection between sports and work is clear: both systems of behavior enhance the status and prestige of the concept of achievement. Accordingly, analogous behavior and consciousness can be expected in both sectors.

3. *The Achievement Principle in Sports and Work*

In an economically organized industrial society, individuals produce goods and services and compete with one another in the marketplace. This fact implies behavior which is oriented toward the achievements of individuals and groups, for individual or collective productive ability determines socioeconomic status. Every action serving economic ends aims at optimal production of truly needed goods and services or at overproduction of goods and services which must be hawked by advertising. This functional interconnection can be illustrated through three objective relationships: (1) Man is a biologically inadequate creature constantly worrying about his physical survival, but the more he produces the more groundless seems his worry. (2) The more extensive his material possessions, the higher his economic and social status. (3) A dogmatic worldview motivates men to increased achievement. This striving for achievement is institutionalized in the world of work and the professions. "The most essential characteristic of the professional system is the primacy of functionally successful achievement. That means that the selection of candidates for a particular position follows from their ability to fulfill certain tasks, i.e., from their innate ability and their education."[1] From the very start, professionally less qualified persons will have lower levels of socially recognized ability attributed to them than to the better qualified. Social status correlates with the degree and the differentiation of the objective occupational achievement. "Every individual occupational category possesses a more or less determined scale for measuring the quality of individual achievement."[2] Typically, we find a quantified hierarchy of occupational roles which express a man's vocational achievement in monetary terms. It seems "unavoidable that pecuniary earnings are commonly taken as the measure of achievement." In this way, an abstract datum functions as the acknowledged symbol of "professional status."[3]

Achievement has thus become a socially sanctioned model of behavior related to high productivity, economic competition, material rewards, vocational practice, and social mobility.

4.   *Top-Level Sports*

Today's fans react with polemics, rage, and even hate when an idolized athlete or team fails to live up to their expectations.[1] The founder of the modern Olympic Games, Pierre de Coubertin, helped bring about this state of affairs when he impressed upon sports the motto *citius, altius, fortius* (faster, higher, stronger). The motto corresponds to "belief in progress and, in the emphasis on achievement, to the principles of industrial society."[2] One simply cannot "do" sports "mildly" and "in moderation," for "in the 'freedom to go all out' is hidden an alluring force," the quest for records. Coubertin sought to justify this force with references to "the power of emulation."[3] Achievement was put forth as a typical characteristic of sport. Achievement "is the most striking essential element in sports . . . : the striving for achievement, for the highest achievement, for records." The desire to set records is remarkable because the athlete voluntarily undertakes fantastic physical efforts that are normally avoided at all costs."[4] Whether one can really speak of "voluntarily" accepted physical effort is quite problematical; the individual who resolves to participate in top-level sports has already subordinated himself to a high degree to the reigning system of values and conventions of behavior. To do top-level sports means to be forced to achieve—in order to fulfill society's expectations of achievement.[5]

In the "theory of physical culture and sports" as it is conceived in the German Democratic Republic [East Germany], top-level sports appear as a social category determined by political and economic factors. "Biological achievement . . . is socially determined. The limits of achievement are set by the development of society and its productive power. Norms of achievement are established by the relevant sciences of medicine and political economy." Physical culture is therefore a "social process of the conscious perfecting of mankind's physical and psychic qualities as an agent of productivity . . ." and also an important sector of socialist society and culture.[6]

Young people identify their own athletic abilities with the specific values of sports. One can see this in the responses to a questionnaire given to students between 10 and 16 years of age at a West German school: a large percentage of the boys affirmed the achievement principle in sports and idolized famous athletes. Among the girls, however, the response was less affirmative.[7]

We have now shown how the concept of achievement has taken on ideological functions in the realm of sports. The next step is to illustrate the sociological and ideological connections between sports and work by describing certain achievement-oriented forms of behavior and consciousness. In doing so, we shall concentrate on top-level sports, by which we mean a complex of social behavior which is directed toward the best possible individual and team athletic achievements. Top-level sports may include both amateurs and professionals. The concept of "social labor" as we use it here refers to individual or collective action, regardless of economic gain, which is directed at maximum achievement. In the products of work, the individual seeks to realize characteristic socially transmitted ideas. A parallel between the products of work and sports can easily be discerned: in both cases, the shaping of individual products appears as the highest goal.

Doing sports and working are both based on human achievement. In sociological terms, "achievement" involves material and nonmaterial values of human behavior which are expressed in factors of optimal qualities or quantities. With respect to achievement, there is a correlation between the orientation of the individual and the expectation of his environment. Unless an athletic achievement meets social expectations, it will not be accepted as such. Similarly, the norms of economic life must be followed if achievements are to be acknowledged as such.

The data of achievement are established, replaced, and administered by the ruling groups of society. They are dissociated quickly from their initiators and, as impersonal institutionalized values, exert a social coercion upon all of us. The objective form of this coercion is the ideology of achievement.

5. "Achievement" A Dominant Model for Behavior in the Behavioral System of Work and Top-Level Sports

In the realm of top-level sport as in that of social labor, the achievement principle dominates. The success of human actions is now measured by the reaching or surpassing of set norms of achievement. Individuals, groups, and institutions are ranked according to their success or failure to achieve. Those who do not strive to fulfill the acknowledged norms of achievement are discredited; they cannot claim high social prestige. The ability to achieve and success in achieving function as the highest social values. It seems almost self-evident that one of the imperatives of modern physical education calls for the best possible individual achievement for any given "psychophysical potential." The relationship of this imperative to the economically defined conception of work is obvious. Thus, the systematic "increase in physical and spiritual stimulus in order to reach the optimal functioning capacity of the organism" is the real goal of athletic training. The connection with the world of work is unambiguous when one of the fundamentals of physical education is that improvements in achievement are possible only "through the planning of the work."[1] Similar formulations appeared long ago in the writings of the efficiency expert F. W. Taylor. Taylor argued that the individual found his greatest "prosperity" in striving for occupational achievement. In other words, "the development of individual capacity to its completest fulfillment enables each individual to attain vocational perfection."[2] Interestingly enough, Taylor uses team sports to exemplify his thesis: every player must seek "to mobilize all his strength to help his team to victory"; if he fails to do this, he "will be scorned by all."[3]

Implicit in both top-level sports and social labor is the demand that we continually raise the level of our achievement. This demand manifests itself in the establishing of goals which are continuously corrected upwardly. The norms of achievement have only provisional validity. "In modern sports' characteristic striving for higher levels of achievement, for records of speed, and for the many-sided development of movement-skills, we can see mirrored the development of modern industrial technology, with all its concomitant demands," namely the demand of the productive sector for particular movement-skills which the worker must provide.[4] Decisive is the optimal occupational achievement, which accounts in turn for optimal production. And this kind of achievement has been adopted from the behavioral model of top-level sports. Peak production and the concept of the record, no matter in what form, no matter in which field of behavior, are typical characteristics of a productivity-oriented, industrial, marketplace society where the most capable competitor receives the best exchange values for his products.

Today, records are no longer set accidentally and without preparation. "In our time, a world record is normally the result of teamwork by scientists, doctors, coaches, masseurs, and sometimes pacers as well as the athletes themselves."[5] Despite this teamwork, scientifically prepared attempts to set records are almost always stymied by human unpredictability, by indecision, and by sudden lapses in ability. A record cannot be wholly planned and predicted. Similar phenomena are observable within the world of work, where individual achievement is increasingly dependent upon collective achievement. While the founders of the great industrial enterprises of the nineteenth and early twentieth centuries were able to rely on their own judgment in assessing the economic situation, today we have specialists concerned with planning, study of the market, analysis of the state of competition. And these specialists often work in teams, taking the place of the omnicompetent activists of earlier times. They create specialized bodies of knowledge, which are the precondition for a general increase in achievement levels. In sports, the 10,000-meter runner is trained and handled by a specialist or even by a staff of specialists. Available data are gathered and analyzed as part of the training program. The top-level athlete has himself become a specialist.

The relationship between the invividual and the society's claim upon his achievements seems on the face of it unproblematical. One assumes all too uncritically that each of us is free to accept or reject society's claim. This kind of freedom may be possible, but it is equally likely that our goals exert normative pressure upon us and that we become dependent upon them in our decisions. Both situations are observable in top-level sports. The athlete determines the norms of achievement he wishes to attain and can alter them when an adjustment of goals seems necessary; on the other hand, the way he behaves is predetermined by the norms of achievement. The training program demands this kind of adjustment to its goals, and carries with it all the implicit consequences of such an adjustment. In addition to systematic preparation, "training for top-level achievement implies the total adaptation of the organism to the top-level achievement and . . . thus to whatever means of training are necessary to make the achievement possible. One's life-style must be subordinated to the development of achievement. . . . Training therefore includes all those measures which are important for preparing the achievement."[6] In short, training is planned behavior "according to which one's entire life is dedicated to approaching one's goal."[7] The top-level athlete—assuming he strives for optimal goals—must therefore adapt himself not only to the training plan but also to prescribed regimens for nourishment, for sleep, and for sexual abstinence. The modern athlete practices the "secular asceticism" described by Max Weber. In the meantime, masochistic tendencies have become obvious; the need to suffer now occurs.[8] The application of force, which is imminent in the whole apparatus of our social behavior, occurs in top-level sports as well. Force which is directed against others becomes force which is directed against oneself as well.

The model for this kind of adaptation is at hand in the capitalist system of production. As long as the producer is also the owner of the means of production, he alone determines the planning and the execution of the work, the length of the work day, and the economic goals of the enterprise. As soon as the producer is reduced to the point where he becomes simply the owner of his own labor power, he is subordinated to criteria established by others. The entire social system of subordination rests on the superior power of the possessor (whether of material or nonmaterial status symbols) over the possessionless person. Nowadays, this relationship is no longer immediately perceivable; it must be discerned in the form of sublimated, impersonal power relationships. The training plan of the top-level athlete and the job descriptions of factors work document them.

The dominant form for comparing achievements is the struggle of competition. Thomas Hobbes saw in competition the originally hostile relationships of the state of nature which the political state, through its force, had regulated and channeled: *homo homini lupus* ["man is a wolf to man"]. In the competitor, one recognizes an adversary whom one must get the better of, against whom one must guard oneself if one wants to survive. This primeval form of human enmity appears in more civilized guise in the exchange relationships of capitalism. Whoever hopes successfully to compete in the marketplace against other producers must, depending on his ability to achieve either labor power or possession of capital, assure himself an optimal share of production or reproduction. High social status is derived from success in the competitive struggle. Thus the competitive struggles become the "second nature" of *Homo faber* ["man the maker"]. This model of behavior for the existential assertion of identity permeates athletic competition too. "One of the most characteristic aspects of contemporary sports is the striving for optimal results which is expressed in athletic competition."[9] This aspect is most obvious in the way that professional sport, a specialized type of high-level sport, has taken over the principle of competition: the most successful in the contest receives the highest remuneration, and the remuneration is the basis of his personal material reproduction.

"Top-level sports occur either during or in relation to a competition in which a comparison of achievement among opponents competing according to objective regulations takes place. The purpose of the contest is the improvement of the level of achievement and the victory over the opponent."[10] The athletic contest is the basis for a system of objectively prepared rules: playing rules, guidelines for contests, classes and divisions of achievement, established sequences of tournaments and championships, rules for material compensation in case of injury. In addition, professional sport brings with it wages, contracts between clubs and athletes and coaches.* The forms of the contest are controlled so that every transgression of the rules is punished. A similar regulation governs the labor market, which is also oriented to norms and scales of compensation: categories of achievement are determined and, once determined, associated with set levels of salaries and wages, and with set rules of the game in the sense of limitations on the kinds of behavior which are accepted in the marketplace. Workers bound by legal contracts are no more to be "tampered with" than the players of a professional soccer club. This achievement-oriented system of interpersonal relationships is embedded in a larger system of rationalized principles of order. "The purpose of the contest is the improvement of the level of achievement and the victory over the opponent." Hobbes's hypothesis is confirmed and extended here as the end and the goal of the athletic contest. The legitimized improvement in the level of achievement is the driving force of successful social action.

In both work and sports, the struggle of competition demonstrates the same socially determined aspects: competition promises gains in personal prestige and in the recognition which follows success in one's occupational activity. For sports clubs, teams, and individuals, a high level of success in sports brings with it positive publicity and a better

---

* Professional sports teams in Germany are sponsored by clubs rather than owned by individuals or corporations. (Trans.)

position in the socially sanctioned hierarchy of achievers. One is worth something in the "achievement marketplace." In other words, the possession of the title or the symbols of an achiever ensures general social recognition. This relationship holds for every kind of occupational achievement; success in the labor or exchange market implies a high social status and a consciousness of one's own ability to achieve.

This kind of rationalization has, of course, a concrete economic basis. Top-level sports are a social enterprise which can assure its quasimaterial reproduction only on the basis of the highest possible achievement. Only repeated achievements can guarantee public recognition and support. And here in the principle of comparative achievement we see the connection between top-level sports and the competitive marketplace: modern sports are "a product of industrial society and symbolize the fundamental principles of that society in concentrated form"; sports, therefore, fascinate "the masses in every industrialized or industrializing land."[11]

Top-level sports and social labor as social subsystems do not present closed and unstructured but rather open and class-structured social forms. One can observe in both subsystems the efficacy of a differentiated hierarchy of achievement according to which "the individuals of any given social system are ranked so that significant social interactions can be conducted through subordination and superordination."[12] Applied to the world of work, this means that the various demands for occupational achievement are simultaneously means of variously

has become quantified."[2] Two problems appear prominent in the analysis of work: the question of improving the so-called "preconditions of achievement," i.e., "measures for raising the efficacy of expended effort," and the question of "the readiness of the worker to achieve during the time of his employment and the effect upon him of alterations in technique or organization."[3]

7. *Complex Methods of Work and Training*

At the handicraft stage of production, the producer unites in his own person all the procedures of production; he is so situated that he can, "up to a certain point, express his occupational experience through skilled behavior."[1] The process of production from raw material to completion is sequential, oriented to the creation of the product. This kind of work is methodologically complex and synthetic or determined by the integrity of the product. The craftsman's own initiative, personal approach to and control over the work, and insight into the nature of the produced object and responsibility for the work performed characterize the handicraft stage of production.

The first stage of training and teaching in modern top-level sports closely resembles this handicraft stage of production. A historical example is useful. In 1896, Robert Garrett, a shot-putter and jumper, was able to win the discus-throw although he had seen a discus for the first time in Athens.[2] The conception of training was originally directed almost exclusively toward the discipline itself, so that 100-meter sprinters ran this stretch in training while soccer players devoted their practice solely to soccer. In short, the structures of handicraft labor lay behind the early methods of training and teaching in sport. One differentiated among athletic skills only in their elementary forms and practiced these in complex training. The high jumper focused on a correct model of the high jump and imitated the whole motion. This sort of training combined personal independence with a lack of motor specialization. The individual athlete developed his own ideas, planned and determined his own goals, and realized them himself. His was the responsibility for the training methods adopted.

8. *Analytical Methods of Work and Training*
Repetitive Processes and Changing Loads

Today's methods of work and training stand in crass contrast to yesterday's holistic methods. The rational planning of work continues to be determined by the produced object, but the process is divided up into the smallest possible segments. No longer can a single person carry out the successive steps leading to the manufacture of the completed product; these steps are now divided or combined into parts and executed with an eye to the optimal use of labor. The complex work process has been atomized. The worker can no longer dispose of his skills; his room for choice has been reduced to a minimum, and he has been relieved of all responsibility for the finished product. Such a pattern of social labor conforms to the laws of increasing productivity and progressive rationalization. The pattern is typical for the sphere of industrial production.

A similar development can be observed in the conception of a modern teaching and training program in top-level sports; the rational planning of athletic behavior dominates. It is true that complex goals determine teaching and training methods, but these goals are broken down into individual parts and phases, which are then carried out either separately or in small sequences. In contrast to the world of work, the individual person still brings together these individual sequences during the "moment of truth" in the contest itself. During the athletic action the rational analysis disappears. Nonetheless, the division-of-labor differentiation of the teaching and training process remains sociologically relevant because the teaching and training process takes up more time than the contest does.

Fundamental principles of a rational training program include the repetitive division of the tasks of training and the law of changing psycho-physical loading, both of which are copied from the methods of industrial labor. Continuous repetition of temporally, spatially, and quantitatively set training tasks, interrupted by controlled pauses for recovery, is exemplified in interval training, the fundamental principle of which is "a periodic (or systematic or cyclic or rhythmic or phased) alternation between exertion and recovery or between work and pause or between heavier and lighter loads." The four corollaries of the principle of interval training are "(1) duration (length of the stretch), (2) tempo (level of the load), (3) intervals or pauses of various lengths and types, (4) number of repetitions." These corollaries are especially valid for middle and distance running but they are applicable in modified form to other disciplines. The goal of interval training is the

increased efficacy of the training. The interval principle is supposed to "make possible a greater amount
of work carried out with greater intensity."[1] Examples are illustrative: "30 × 100 meters in 15.5-16.5
seconds," "1-minute pause"; "15 × 200 meters in
30-31 seconds," "90-second pause"; "3 × 2,000
meters in 5:51.4 minutes," "in 5:51.0 minutes," "in
5:57.5 minutes," each time "3-minute pause."[2]
Translated, this means that a runner must run 100
meters thirty separate times with a one-minute pause
between each run, during which pauses he must not
rest but must jog further.[3]

The principle of repetition and of changing loads
is obvious. It is no longer left up to the individual
athlete to decide how he will train. With "tayloris-
tic" strictness, the exact plan "replaces the thinking
process of the individual worker" or athlete.[4] Training, comparable now to assembly-line production,
takes place in "more or less simple operations performed at regular intervals."[5] Just as in the organization of industrial work, pauses are planned with
the intention to "figure in the hidden usefulness of
'empty time' between the separate moments of the
work process [or training program] so that greater
productivity can be achieved." In work just as in
sports, "the rationalized interval becomes 'the pause
that pays' in both senses of the word. Disguised as
play and as the voluntary unleashing of one's energies, sports simply duplicate the world of work."[6]
The training that one must accomplish is as coer-
cively outlined as the work that must be done on the
assembly line, which "gives the worker guidelines

with whose help he can at any time measure his progress and whose fulfillment offers him the greatest
pleasure."[7]

The examples of training given above, with their
formal division into quantified units of repetitions,
distances, times, and pauses, demonstrate a direct
connection with the industrial speed-up combined
with the promise of higher pay. Both systems of behavior can be subsumed under the concept of assembly line production planned as a "smoothly flowing
series of operations performed on the basis of the
division-of-labor, bound together in one place, and
carried out sequentially."[8] Even more expressive is
the French expression *travail à la chaine* [chain
labor] applied to the characteristics of assembly line
production; like the links of a chain, the same work
is done over and again: this is a chain in a second
sense as well, for the worker is shackled to a set sequence of repetitive actions. A similar method, also
using the principle of repetition and of changing
loads, leads to the adoption of so-called circuit training. Within a "circle" are a number of "stations,"
each with its specific task to be accomplished. At
each station, one does the prescribed exercise (weight-
lifting, knee-bends, sit-ups, etc.). No pauses are per-
mitted between the stations, aside of course from the
time required to go from one to another. As a rule,
the "trainee" begins with one round of the circle and
increases the number of rounds according to his individual capacity. As an illustration, a circle might
consist of (1) "climbing a bench or box and stepping
along it," (2) "crouching and hopping in and out of

push-up position," (3) "jumping and chinning," etc. The number of repetitions will vary according to the individual. In looking more closely into circuit training, we can make out the familiar factors of repetitive work: a precise number of repetitions for each movement, psycho-physical load-changing, formal ordering of the exercises to be accomplished, directions for motor behavior. In short, we see how the trainee is bound to a definite plan of labor. The methodical elements of circuit training remind one of manufacturing methods still used for products which cannot be economically produced by assembly line techniques. For instance, suppose a worker must put together 100 pieces of a given object. A number of approaches are possible: he may bore the required holes in every object (first station), bend the objects into an angle (second station), smooth all sharp edges (third station), etc. He may also repeat the circle more often by preparing only 10 pieces at a time, thus going through the circle 10 times. In both situations, circuit training and manufacturing series, we see the characteristic marks of a variety of operations performed at the standardized stations of a work or training process.

The practice of modern tactical team training is not structurally different from the general tendency to imitate rationalized, work-like patterns of behavior in the realm of top-level sports. The concept of action on the basis of movements analyzed into elementary steps which are mastered one at a time has become the mode in training for ball games. Offensive and defensive systems are abstracted from their total context and isolated and practiced as continually repeated maneuvers until they become a matter of habit. The literature is full of examples of strictly schematized plays in which each player has his role: "G passes to G' and screens. G' dribbles and passes to F. G' screens for F. F passes to G and screens for him. G. passes to C and drives by. G' cuts behind G and by C on a natural four-way block, receiving a pass from C."[10] Any player who seeks to break out of the tactical system will be—at least during training—forced by the coach to return to the behavioral stereotype. In the contest itself, the pattern of socialized behavior is applied in complex plays and can even be improvised. In contrast to the narrowly determined, analytical demands of work, the playing field offers the possibility for independent solutions to problems. Nonetheless, the break-it-into-parts method of tactical team training remains the basis for learning game behavior. In training, team sports copy the forms of the division of labor even if the analytical scheme can be set aside during the contest itself so that new solutions to specific playing situations can be found.

Criticism of the training methods described above has barely begun. It is revealing that the criticism agrees on many points with the criticism of the division of labor in industry and of the consequences of that division of labor, and this despite the outward dissimilarity of sports and work. Trainer P. W. Cerutty's objection that the so-called "scientific training" is really a "pseudoscientific training" parallels Georges Friedmann's complaint against the scientific status of the technocratic system invented by F. W. Taylor, namely, that "the system of fixed plans is developed out of the training process without allowing any choice to the athlete himself. The plan is predetermined and it is simply assumed that the athlete will follow the plan."[11]

A comparative criticism of methods of rationalization in top-level sports and in industrial work leads, as has already been demonstrated, to similar points: interval training and assembly line work can both be described as repressive (in Friedmann's terms "rigid") systems of behavior guidelines which constrict to a minimum the individual's space for choosing and behaving. The "human factor" (Friedmann) is incorporated into the technocratic training or labor planning. Freidmann speaks of "removing the soul from work."[12] Theodor Adorno writes that sports give man back a "part of the functions which the machine has deprived him of," but "only so that men may be even more remorselessly placed at the service of the machine. Sports begin even to turn the body into a machine."[13] This development turns the rationalizing process into the opposite of its original intention, which was to raise achievement and productivity, for it has been empirically established that "excessively small units of work lead to boredom, unhappiness, and even to a decline in achievement."[14] One cause of such a decline is surely monotony. In circumstances where optimally divided and barely structured tasks follow quickly one upon the other, consciousness can no longer see meaning in the situation. "There is no more individual 'now' that can be related to a 'before' and an 'after.' The subject places himself nowhere in time but rather experiences only a sense of duration. . . . The reduction of the temporary dimension of a situation to a feeling of mere duration—that is the fact of monotony."[15] This danger threatens wherever the rational division of activity and the reduction of the situation to "mere duration" occurs, in athletic training as well as in the forms of industrial work. Sports' claim to fulfill a function which is contrary to that of work is no longer tenable, for here too rationalized techniques have been introduced which lead to monotonously schematized behavior and to the dissolution of consciously experienced temporal structure. As Jürgen Habermas expresses it, top-level sports appear "long since to have become an aspect of the rationalization of labor."[16] The history of the division of labor demonstrates an oscillation between complex and simple activities."[17] Athletic training methods today are going through a similar change. If track-and-field training methods up to 1960 emphasized the analytically conceived interval method for middle and distance runners, now there is a tendency to switch to the more complexly conceived principle of duration—i.e., a temporally and spatially looser kind of training over longer stretches. It is historically relevant for research into the connections between sport and work that top-level sports originated in the phase of the industrial division of labor. With the progressive "splintering of work'' (Friedmann) sports took on work-like training and teaching methods—at any rate, after a certain time-lag. Genetically, however, it is clear that sports rose in a causal, social, historical relationship with the industrial development of rationalized human labor.

9. *Dismembering Teaching Methods*

In modern athletic training and physical education, the learning process is divided up like the division of labor into single movements and elements of behavior which are practiced in isolation and which the student must later bring together in complete actions. Methodical workout sequences have been developed, routines based on the principles of physical education. The purpose is to facilitate the mastering of particular motor and social tasks in a step-by-step manner. For example, one doesn't learn to throw the discus immediately but masters the different parts of the throwing sequence and learns progressively to put all the parts together. The same is true for games where tactics are learned one at a time and then brought together into complete systems of social behavior.

Teaching methods in sport are modeled after the apprenticeship system of craft and industrial production. The skills to be learned are divided up into their elements, which the apprentice must master step by step according to their increasing difficulty. For example, "smoothing" must be learned in stages beginning with planing of even surfaces and ending with complicated shaping of uneven surfaces. In sports, as in the craft and industrial systems of vocational education, the principle of repetition of tasks is as important as the principle of division of skills for inculcating stereotypical behavior. Such a form of the learning and teaching process is actually based on the rules of the game in market competition. There is reason to suspect that these rules apply even within the world of pedagogy.

10. *Timing and Bureaucratizing*

The rational dismemberment of the contents of social labor and top-level sports implies a goal-oriented planning of their temporal dimensions. Training programs and work plans are both subjected to exact timing. One consequence of this is that the top-level athlete cannot train according to his own time plan. Every arbitrary and spontaneously carried out athletic activity is constricted to fit the training plan. F. W. Taylor's prognosis seems as valid for top-level sports as for industrial labor: "Up to now, personality came first; from now on, organization and system take over."[1] It is no different for the laborer: his hours are determined by his employer. In both sports and work, the individual is literally at someone's employ during the period of productive activity. It is not simply the work day which is shaped and fixed; the future too has its training programs and work plans designed according to specific goals (setting athletic and industrial records). A scientifically based training program encompasses weeks, months, and even years. Theorists of training speak of "daily training plans" (mornings and afternoons), "weekly training plans," "yearly plans," "long-range plans."[2] During such periods the individual athlete or the team is "built up" or "constructed" to reach the desired level of achievement just as an economic concern is devoted to reaching an optimal level of production. Athletic training programs clearly show the traces of rationalized, goal-oriented, planned behavior.

Rationalization assumes logically necessary forms when it goes on to become bureaucratization and administration of top-level sports. One can perceive the influence of bureaucratic principles in the following phenomena: the growth of sport bureaucracy which exercises a limited rule on the basis of its power to make decisions; the acceptance of the principle of functional bureaucratization as described by Max Weber so that an "intensive and qualitative expansion and unfolding of the sphere of responsibility of administration" takes place under the leadership of experts acting with conceptually systematized and rationalized legal and semilegal authorization.[3] Bureaucratization is a necessary aspect of modern sports' rationalization, for the increase in the numbers of those "doing" sports has diminished the opportunities for them to "do" sport freely and without formal organization.[4] After a certain point a number of interests and groups oppose each other in a way that demands legitimized regulation. Special sports bureaucracies, distinguished by their "drawing up of rules, by their delimiting competences and thereby the order of relationships," act to provide the member with structure and order," for instance, by laying out the member's rights and duties. The sports bureaucracy undertakes the tasks of administration.[5] In West Germany, the German Sport Federation (*Deutscher Sportbund*—DSB) has these bureaucratic functions. In the DSB the various associations for the different disciplines (e.g., the soccer or ski associations) come together in an all-encompassing organization. The following division of jurisdictions has developed (sketched out roughly here): the DSB administers, programs, and represents the interests and goals of all sports while the various associations have delegated responsibilities. The overall organization and the specialized ones act as pressure groups which incorporate a definite ideological position vis-à-vis top-level sports and its functional categories. The position manifests itself in specific regulations: establishing norms of achievement (e.g., entry qualifications), codifying tables of achievement for calculating athletic achievements, formulating administrative regulations for competitions, dividing competitors into classes; and in addition, regulating the relationships among sports clubs and associations, creating an internal judicial system to oversee the associations' constitutions and punish violations of them, nominating national teams, and employing scientists and trainers concerned for research into training methods for the improvement of achievement.

Just as in the bureaucratized world of work, various interest groups come into conflict: the administrators versus the administered. In sports as well as in work, a typical model of our social system appears: the rule of a bureaucratic organization administered by a small group of administrators. Obviously, this new bureaucratic system "lays a large measure of responsibility on the shoulders of the administration" and constricts the degree of choice left to the individual.[6] The work world experiences a similar constriction of the economic initiatives of the individual on the part of associations acting to establish norms of behavior, kinds and quantities of production, wage and price scales, work rules, etc.

The bearers of the burden of the above-mentioned bureaucratic forms are the sports association and the economic organization, respectively. Both institutions develop and enforce administrative measures which are structurally and functionally analogous. In both cases we have a "cooperative social system" demanding "the exercise of numerous activities characterized by the division of labor. The activities must be subordinated to the goals of the enterprise, which calls for a system of directions and controls. From these necessities grows a hierarchically organized, formally defined system of technical-organizational functions."[7] The interactions within a sports club demonstrate the division of labor within the framework of a fixed, formal organization. Hierarchically organized offices interact according to precisely defined responsibilities. These offices constitute the executive committee of the club within which various office-holders devise committees to deal with special problems and tasks. There is also a "legislature" consisting of all members having the right to vote. The legislature determines the goals of the club and elects the various officers. A written club constitution codifies the club's "laws," whose enforcement is watched over by a special court or judiciary. Branches and sections based on the various sports disciplines are founded and divide the club into sectors which, like its model the industrial enterprise, can possess a certain independence within the overall structure of the club. Also, the erection of administrative advisory committees staffed by administrative experts from public posts and from private enterprise, both serving in an advisory capacity, characterizes a development which in the largest sports clubs approaches that of the administered sports industry. All these marks of a technical-organizational framework have long since distinguished the basic structure of the capitalistic economic system and have been transferred from capitalism to other areas of rationalized behavior. In fact, bureaucratization appears today as a benchmark of industrial society and its division of labor. Bureaucratization has developed the specific techniques of goal-oriented, rationally planned rule. Bureaucracy means here more than simply a "means to run an organization."[8] Every aspect of social life is now subordinated to planned administration. The result is that bureaucracy constantly narrows the individual's room for choice. And top-level sports have long since taken this step to administered sports.

11. *The Work-Like Role-System of Top-Level Sports*

The bureaucratization of top-level sports implies a system of social roles like that existing in the world of work. Within a sports club, as in an industrial enterprise, every active person acquires a rank that fixes his area of activity. In a goal-oriented, social, behavioral apparatus, such a status is precisely defined. Depending on its goals, tasks, and responsibilities, every enterprise creates subordination and superordination by the structure of its roles. "Formal social organization is . . . a system of social roles related hierarchically and organized to make possible the fulfillment of the goals of the enterprise."[1] Every social role is linked on the basis of objective determinations to expected behavior on the part of those who fill the role.

Top-level sports have copied this model of ordered status and roles in their elementary forms of social organization. Like the director of an economic enterprise the president of a sports club (or the chairman of its executive committee) incorporates the highest level of control and decision-making. He speaks authoritatively, utters the principles of club politics, and appears in public as representative of the club. When there are conflicts of interest with other institutions, he acts as the negotiating go-between. In his leadership role, one expects to find typical qualities in him—e.g., specialized information, rhetorical ability, identification with the tasks to be accomplished, and organizational tact. The president of a sports club can be seen as a general manager who exercises a high-level coordinating function within the club management. Alongside of him stand the experts whose spheres of activity are objectively determined: the vice-president (or second officer) who is responsible for administration and organization, the director of sports and play who coordinates the whole field of athletic activity, the press secretary, the treasurer, and such yet more specialized roles as legal advisor. These roles correspond to those of the directors of an industrial enterprise. Every division of a sports club has its chief whose functions match those of the superintendent or divisional manager of a business firm. He carries out the directions of his superiors in the management and acts independently to accomplish the tasks delegated to him. The margin of independence for the divisional leader of a sports club is, however, greater than that in an economic enterprise because, in most cases, the former is an unpaid volunteer within an athletic organization whose existence is not primarily goal-oriented nor dependent on successful decisions. There is no strictly formal set of regulations. On the other hand, the role of the athletic trainer is like that of the top-level athlete himself—clearly determined by goal-oriented norms which define their status and the characteristics of their position—the characteristics, that is, of specialized knowledge, practical mastery of the specific athletic discipline, leadership characteristics such as empathy with the psychic situation of an athlete, ability to assume group leadership, capacity to make objective decisions. In short, the trainer must have personal and objective prerequisites enabling him to direct training at the optimal level of achievement in order to accomplish the central goal of the specialist. In the United States there are team sports (baseball, American football, basketball) with trainers solely responsible for the physical conditioning of the team while the head coach and his assistants teach strategy and prepare the players for the contest itself.

The role of the top-level athlete himself, like that of the worker and the employee, is based on his promise of specific achievement. One expects achievement-oriented behavior from him: training (work), industry, punctuality, fulfillment of the training tasks (work quotient), etc. All these expectations are normally written up in the form of a formal pledge or a professional contract, which fixes the role and is binding on the signatories.

Team sports offer the most typical example of the division-of-labor role system in sport. In the descriptions of the individual playing positions, one can see quite explicitly the definitions of the roles: "middle stormer," "right runner," "left defender," "goalies," etc. These names determine a spatial bounding of the field upon which the game takes place (e.g., the goalie), a prescribed function for each player (e.g., defenseman), or a specific role-expectation (a forward). Every description of the position contains a catalogue of characteristics which imply a prescribed pattern of behavior for the individual player. Differentiated roles appear, but not in isolation one from another; they appear within the team as part of a system of roles. Teamwork is the guiding principle. Nowadays, socially and politically progressive industrial firms look upon the sociological concept of teamwork as a model of effective work organization.

12. *Team-Like and Structure-Like Cooperation*

We can speak of cooperation among teammates or coworkers when their activity "is immediately conditioned by and guided by others so that the individual must explicitly consider others in order to complete his own activity."[1] An example of this is to be found in the work technique of a group of laborers in the steel industry; according to empirical investigation, the observed workers must drive trucks loaded with earth to a furnace. They are not bound to any particular work patterns and can divide the work up as they prefer so long as they fulfill their established quota. They are able to support each other, since their individual tasks are not in conflict. On the basis of the binding work rules and the tasks to be done, an "indirect dependence" developed among the workers.[2] The cooperation of a sports team rests on a similar structure: the individual player is not bound to set behavior and can, in most playing situations, decide on his own tactics; but he is subjected to regulations about playing time and the amount and duration of training. Since playing maneuvers are not related to each other deterministically, there is room for spontaneous "assists" and thus for a widening of the role of player. Along with the pressure of binding role expectations, the common goals of the game exert an integrating social pressure upon the whole team. Upon this basis of limited, rational role-planning in sports and in work, the organizing principle of teamwork allows an individual a choice of actions. In other words, an informal system of roles exists along with the formal one.

However, with the intensifying of technical-organizational-rationalizing measures, there frequently occurs in many behavioral situations a progressive diminution of the individual's freedom to act. This has led to the creation of "structural cooperation," the characteristics of which can be read from the above-mentioned example in the steel industry: the work force cooperates "in a kind of detour around the technical structure" because most activities are designed to be done with mechanical devices.[3] Consequently, every worker has "his own set work place, and in this work place his own specialized, clearly outlined functions."[4] He can no longer decide freely among possible activities because the temporal order of work has been specified and there is no possibility for mutual help. Cooperation now means "the division of labor and technically conditioned cooperative work."[5] One can observe a similar development in modern team play: instead of the "technical structure" of the factory we have a rational conception of tactics which coerces the individual player into habits of predetermined cooperation. The very conception of a team places every player into a set place with specialized and precisely prescribed tasks (for example, to block an opponent from achieving *his* game plan). Arbitrary decisions are no longer possible. Spontaneous "assists" are intentionally made more difficult because they carry with them the danger of the neglect of obligatory tasks. Teamwork has been subordinated to purposeful rational planning, which transforms team play into a kind of tactically determined cooperation based upon the division of labor. The players' interaction is thus mediated by a structure of tactical rules.

Contemporary practice does show a tendency, however, to free team play from the extreme limitations placed upon individual movement. The key figure is not the narrow specialist but rather the "all-round player." He has the capacity, depending on the structure of the situation, to fill various playing roles. A soccer player can, for instance, in the so-called 4-2-4 or 4-3-3 systems, alternate between "right defender" and "left outer stormer."* This flexibility corresponds to Georges Friedmann's concept of an improvement of assembly line production by having the individual worker learn different "parts of the work in order to shift from one to another. . . . The circulation of workers under this system has increased productivity beyond the classical methods of individual, specialized tasks."[6] The gain can be traced to "a change of pace," "a work rhythm that

---

* Or, in baseball terms, a right-fielder who can also play first base. [Trans.]

isn't bound to the conveyor belt," "greater demands for initiative and dexterity," "less physical weariness," and [social] mobility.[7] The observed higher level of achievement in team play under the all-round system can doubtless be traced to the same arguments.

13. *Technical Rationality— a Hallmark of Modern Sports*

Modern sports were born in the nineteenth century during the transformation of work from handicraft techniques to those of the factory and the industrial system. At that time, track and field sports, swimming, rowing, soccer, and other disciplines were developed and organized in England—history's first industrial society. These sports appeared as regulated contests. With techniques drawn from industrial production and from the unfolding world of capitalistic market relationships, modern sports constituted themselves first as a noneconomic sort of competitive behavior. In the meantime, however, technological development has made such great strides "that human contacts outside the world of work are always accompanied by a third party, that is, by technology with its structures" and machines. Technology inserts itself into social structures and not only modifies them but simultaneously reshapes them.[1] Industrial society has created a technological consciousness which in turn conditions the shape of the nontechnological realms of behavior.

For modern top-level sports, numbers—with all

the weight of their technical-rational symbolism—
have assumed a central significance. By the media-
tion of numbers, the results of training or of contests
can be expressed quantitatively: scores of games,
times of races, distances for throwing and jumping,
etc. Beneath the numbers lies the attempt to find a
scheme for "calculating life."[2] In numbers, the wish
is expressed to present every phenomenon in terms
of equivalence. Every "incomparable" is made comparable because it is "reduced to its abstract dimensions."[3] Top-level sports adopt the principle of "ac-
countability" from realm of exchange relationships.
In doing so, sports take part in the "ever more clearly
observable rationalization of our lives on the model
of the contemporary natural sciences; sports reject
the qualitative in order to embrace the measured and
quantified." Sports are no longer means for education; "quantification and the measurement of
achievements have become the very substance of
sports."[4] "Side by side with the value of the mere
experience is the quantified achievement, the objectified thing that it's all about."[5] Sports are now concerned chiefly with "firsts" and with breaking records. The equaling of a record is felt merely as the
repetition of an already achieved quantity.

The tendency to present athletic achievements
through the medium of numbers is mirrored in the
adoption of the same units of measurement used in
the world of work. Athletic achievements now take
place in the "objective framework" of the c-g-s (centimeter, gram, second) system or in point scores
which rely either upon objectively measurable

achievements (as in the pentathlon and decathlon) or in referees' calls and subjective judgments (as in team games, gymnastics, boxing, etc.). The application of a socially sanctioned system of measurement allows the objective comparison of all athletic achievements—exactly like the achievements of labor productivity. They are all rationalized into universally understandable measurements of value. With such quantified, abstract forms, it is possible to compete even against opponents who are not present. One may race, for example, against a world record. In such an attempt, the aspirant may compete independently from the other contestants, who are present merely for formality's sake (i.e., I.A.A.F. rules) or to serve as a pacemaker.

The organizers of top-level sports have no intention of ignoring practicality and giving up the numerically set units of measurements in favor of the only alternative: establishing a rank order (first, second, third, etc.) without calculating exact times or distances on an interval scale of minutes and seconds or meters and centimeters. (The Greeks, however, have been shown by historical research to have used just that alternative at their Olympic games.) In this industrial era, which has brought forth top-level sports, the use of the unaided eye seems absurd and impractical. Our consciousness is quantitative. The modern Olympic games could accordingly be transformed into a spectacular festival of numbers without any ideological resistance on the part of the Olympic functionaries. The Olympic national standings are a tabular synopsis of the index of national

athletic success as expressed in medals, which are
in turn the quantified statement of placings. The
standings have taken on functions similar to the comparison of the production statistics of competing national economies and have led to similarly deduced
ideological misinterpretations. The political, economic, and other struggles of the world's peoples
appear in sublimated forms in the stadium.

The technical conditions of top-level sports are
also expressed in the standardized equipment used
in the contest. One cannot compete with whatever
equipment is closest to one's heart—at least not in official contests. Such sports facilities as tracks, swimming pools, and ballfields are also subject to specified spatial dimensions. Sports events cannot take
place just anywhere; they take place only under
standardized circumstances. Anyone who insists
upon using his own irregular equipment or unmea-
sured stretches and places simply excludes himself
from the system of comparable measures of achievement. The norming of sports equipment and facilities
also has parallels in the world of work, where the
standardization of all the conditions of production
and competition has been striven for. Today, the
times and distances of athletic achievements are
measured with the aid of stopwatches, tapemeasures,
crossbars, optically constructed distance measures,
anomometers, film and photo apparatus, mobile
carts, etc. "In this exact measuring of fractions of
seconds we find the characteristic control of time
and temporal organization which is peculiar to the
technical age."[6]

The machine, symbol of the marriage of human labor and technology, has in the meantime forced its way into many areas of top-level sports; the machine appears—roughly put—in two forms: (1) simple, tool-like devices with a primarily instrumental character that serve to extend athletic activities and physical skills (starting machines, vaulting poles, weight-training machines, trampolines, bicycles, bats, tennis rackets, and hockey sticks); (2) non-human-powered equipment (automobiles, motorcycles, airplanes, motorboats).

The machine is adapted to the performer, the performer to the machine. In the latter case, men have adapted themselves to the machine after having first fled *from* the mechanization of industrial labor *to* the world of sports where the machine, in a figurative sense, followed them.

With the integration of technical instruments into top-level sports, sports become partially dependent upon the whole process of technological development. Some—auto racing, gliding, scuba diving—are simply impossible without special technical equipment. Achievement in these disciplines is obviously inseparable from the development of well constructed, high-quality instruments. The progress of achievement in many sports has been greatly accelerated by technical discoveries and innovations. Where a polevault of 4.80 meters was considered excellent a decade ago, now [1968] one is catapulted more than 50 centimeters higher, thanks to the fiberglass pole. This fact reminds us of the economic production process, whose efficacy in producing goods and services is continually heightened by technological progress. New sports disciplines (trampoline contests, go-cart races, bobsled runs) follow upon the invention of new devices. There are new disciplines for which muscular strength and motor coordination and stamina are less important than fine motor coordination and the capacity for psychological concentration (target shooting, golf, table-tennis). This restructuring of the demands upon the body has been studied by Georges Friedmann through the examples of industrial work, where the demand for fine muscular coordination is continually rising. A similar tendency in sports, coupled with progress in achievement levels and with human inventiveness, brings the development of new types of motor skills and technical sports equipment. There is a parallel development of new patterns of behavior.

The concept of "technique" in modern sports can also be indirectly related to human behavior because every sports discipline has its specific techniques. Purposeful athletic movements are called movement technique. For each technique there is a prescribed, optimally economic (time-, distance-, or energy-conserving) sequence of movement. In this sense, technique means something like a normative, purposeful mode of movement. "It is unmistakable that the development stands in close relationship to progressive mechanization and that sports themselves are becoming ever more mechanical. We see this . . . even in the disciplines from which machines have been formally excluded, such as boxing, wrestling, swimming, running, jumping, throwing, putting. Man himself has become a kind of machine whose movements, controlled by his equipment, are mechanical."[7] If human movements are to be forced into purposeful, rational frameworks, a technocratic conception of athletic activity must appear on the scene.

14. The "Scientification" of Top-Level Sports and Work

"Scientification," the highest stage in the rationalizing of work, is the instrumental application of scientific methods in actual practice. Taylor's thesis that "there is a science in the worker's smallest action"[1] is the basis for a technical-analytical science of work conceived with a system-stabilizing (functional) intention. The goal of this science is to use exact research into human labor in order to increase productivity. This goal can be reached "when all unnecessary motion is eliminated, when slow movements are replaced by fast ones, when uneconomic grips and holds are replaced by economic ones."[2] Taylor's student, F. B. Gilbreth, made the connections between labor-power expenditure and labor time more precise in his book *Motion and Time Study*. "First the dimension of space and then that of time must be announced. The goal orientation and the success of work are obviously related first to the shape and then to the tempo of the movement." Gilbreth observed the "laziest" worker and "learned from him the most economical movements and took him . . . as a model."[3] Every effort at the scientific study of human labor in industrial work situations serves, finally, the purpose of raising levels of achievement. Precisely at this point we can see the similarity to developments in the scientific analysis of top-level sports: The aim of movement studies in top-level sports is to arrange for sequences of motion which are "ever more purposeful, rational, and therefore successful."[4] Accordingly, the laws of human movement in sports are sought out and transformed into rational rules for movement. Spatial and temporal dimensions of athletic movement become from this point of view the objects of scientific consideration just as did the movements of work. Athletic movement is seen in terms of "the energistic postulate" (Taylor), by which is meant energy-saving actions within a purposeful system of behavior. Research into both top-level sports and work is always done with an eye to the "best possible work procedures" (H. Hilf) or to the optimal technique of athletic motion. Gilbreth himself recognized an affinity between work and sports in this common effort at efficiency; he remarked that "the theory and practice of the single best sort [meaning the optimal work or training procedure] in sports is identical with that of the single best sort in the work process, in every branch of the economy, and in every kind of work."[5]

In both realms of behavior, the "best" method is based on scientific observation and the evaluation of such factors as movement, time, ability, and fatigue. It is striking how both work and sports agree upon the research methods to be employed in their studies: observation, photography, light-traces, com-

binations of cinematographic and dynamographic methods, achievement and motion tests, etc. It is noteworthy that two such apparently different fields can be researched through the same methods. The reason is doubtless that both fields are structured in the same way. Our suspicions to this effect are supported by the fact that both the life of work and that of top-level sports display analogous basic forms of motion: "Movements which men transfer directly to other objects in order to move them (lifting, pushing, pressing)"; "movements by which men utilize specific tools for the indirect transfer of movements to the object in order to heighten their efficacy and increase the radius of their action" (golf clubs or tennis rackets).[6]

Sports psychology too has examined these interrelationships which, according to K. Kohl, are recognizable

when we pay attention to the activities themselves and to the forces, physical and psychological, responsible for the complete achievement: (1) the required achievement often lies on the frontier of the individual's capacity for achievement; (2) external and internal conditions (e.g., fatigue) influence the achievement; (3) skills must be learned as special techniques; (4) speed or precision (or both at once) are called for; (5) a reaction is often required because of a stimulus (signal), simple or complex in nature, from the environment; (6) exact cooperation is necessary with regards to a common goal and difficulties appear because the partners are not "broken in" to each other; (7) the activities can be simple completing actions, but are also continuing actions that must be continually planned in advance. Among factors of this sort, which influence athletic achievements, we can observe those which contribute to the increase or decrease in the level of achievement at work.[7]

To this argument one might add that the forms of action in top-level sports and in work can in terms of motion, complement each other. A study of the "movement of sports" can "contribute a great deal to the improvement of observation of the motions of work and thus to vocational education.[8]

15. *Top-Level Sports as a Commodity*

The purpose of the following digression is to test the degree to which the existing forms of top-level sports can be analyzed with the categories of Marxist sociology. We begin with the assumption that the social phenomena of a capitalistically oriented exchange society can be made transparent, i.e., can be clarified through an analysis of the structure of commodities. The commodity as an object contains stored within it data relevant to the entire complex process of production and exchange of commodities and all the associated socioeconomic behavioral systems and power relationships. By "commodity" we mean an external "object, a thing that by nature of its attributes satisfies some sort of human need."[1] An object becomes a commodity or an article of exchange only when it is something produced not to satisfy the producer's needs but to be exchanged in the marketplace for other values (money). The question is, can top-level sports bring forth values that we can usefully define as commodity-like? Do top-level sports follow the principles of an exchange society? If one observes a sports event with these questions in mind, one sees evidence of the following social relationships: two groups face one another; the athlete achieves, while the spectators view the athletic competition in order to satisfy their own needs. The athlete is the producer, the spectators the consumers. The athlete's achievement is transformed into a commodity and is exchanged on the market for its equivalent value, expressed in money. This exchange is fully independent of the question of whether the participating producer is a professional or an amateur athlete. In either event the spectator-consumer receives the material object called for. Indeed, the professional receives a cash income regulated by contract and the amateur receives compensation for privately incurred expenses (as regulated by the statutes of the sports associations). At any rate, the official regulations are no longer strictly enforced, which has led to a situation in which amateurs today still differ from professionals in their material status, but not by much. The ideal of the pure amateur in top-level sports has long since become a myth.

The individual achievement of the individual athlete is quantitatively measured and also takes on the attributes of a commodity. According to his quantitatively measured athletic ability at any given time (the special quality of his labor power), the athlete is worth a certain amount in the player-market of professional sports. High transfer or compensation sums must be paid by buyers (sports clubs or the interests backing them) when they want to purchase an athlete. As bearers of scarce and sought after qualities, men turn themselves into commodities. The raising of young rookies in such market circumstances is a profitable undertaking for the sports club. In Europe, these economic relationships occur predominantly in international professional soccer, although similar if officially tabu market rules have come to govern top-level amateur sports as well. A star amateur performer's high market value expresses itself, for example, in the form of offers to turn professional. In buying up highly qualified athletes, an economically powerful sports club is motivated less by material considerations than by a desire for greater prestige.* In this case, a professional soccer club might finance an economically costly track-and-field branch which serves to enhance its public image as an institution dedicated to sports. This entire mechanism for the exchange of commodities appears in its ideal form in the world of work and has been adapted from there and applied to top-level sports; extraordinary athletic ability is either the basis for an exchange of commodities or is itself turned into a commodity.

The production and consumption of commodities implies also a process of reproduction. "No society can continue to produce, i.e., reproduce, without continually reinvesting a part of the product into the means of production or into elements of new production."[2] Reproduction can be understood as physical regeneration; when the producer uses up his labor power and exchanges it for its material equiv-

* In the United States, most professional teams are motivated by profit rather than prestige. See Roger Noll, ed., *Government and the Sports Business* (Washington, 1974). [Trans.]

alent, which he then consumes to satisfy his material needs, he ensures his continued physical existence. He acts simultaneously as producer and reproducer. "Every societal production process is simultaneously a reproduction process if considered in its steady state and in the continuous flow of its renewal."[3] This model can also be verified in the case of top-level sports: the athlete produces an achievement and exchanges it for its monetary equivalent, which he then uses to ensure his own existence and the regeneration of the physical self which, in turn, produces new achievements. He unites in one person the characteristics of producer and reproducer. One might also say that the production of athletic achievements acts in reverse to include the reproduction of the prerequisites of the achievements. Among professionals, this circle of purposeful, rational, economic behavior is obvious. In top-level amateur sports the connections are more ambiguous: There are reimbursements for expenses, useful prizes, and sub-rosa cash payments, but athletic achievements are also indirectly related to educational opportunities, vocational positions, military ranks, and thus to the possibility of upward social mobility. In this way, reproduction becomes the improvement of social status without being directly expressed in monetary terms. For example, many former stars "retire" to managerial positions in business (a very common occurrence in the United States) or they use their athletic winnings to go into business for themselves.

Just as in the world of work, we can observe two

competing groups in the circulation of athletic production and reproduction: the producers of athletic achievement vie with the owners of capital (promoters, managers), who offer athletic exhibitions as commodities in a special market. The relations between the two interest groups are based on the recognized rules of an exchange society: optimal capacity for achievement is exchanged for the prevailing market price.

When human labor power is reduced to an abstract commodity human behavior is reified. Interpersonal relationships based on the exchange of commodities become measurable, formalized objects. This phenomenon appears as markedly in sports as in the social world of work. The ability of a professional athlete is expressed in monetary terms: for every extraordinary achievement, a bonus is paid, every professional possesses a changing market value, and the top-level amateur is offered an adequate basis for reproduction. In this way, every activity is expressed in universally understandable forms which also have distinct effects as social symbols; they serve as a normative scale of values to which every kind of behavior can be subordinated; they function according to set goals. Because of their abstractness, however, they say little about the personal qualities of the producer; one speaks in sports of a "9.9-second-man," a million-dollar ballplayer, a "53-second-freestyler," etc. Behind these quantifications, the living human, with his special qualities, disappears. The fans are less interested in the individual characteristics of the athletes than in their quantifiable abilities, that are turned into functions, factors in spectacular athletic events. Similarly, the characteristic qualities of a worker are of little interest within the productive process while his measured, normative labor capacity is uppermost. This observation leads directly into the problem of the self-realization of the individual through his productiveness. "A working man expresses his individuality and uniqueness in the product of his labor and preserves his free personality through this creative process. Human labor is both the guarantee of individual development and of social progress."[4]

Top-level sports permit self-development within certain boundaries. The narrower the limits of any given system of athletic behavior, the less the chance for self-realization. There is little tolerance for the individual shaping of a 100-meter dash or the lifting of a barbell. This fact can be related to the concept of alienation.[5] The worker no longer disposes independently of his skills; he carries out parts of the work process and can see only a limited sector of the whole. The indications of alienation begin to appear in top-level sports when the individual discipline declines into a highly specialized activity or when rationalized training methods are used, e.g., interval training, which coerces the athlete into continual repetition of the same precisely fixed and isolated narrow tasks.

This reification of productive behavior into a commodity brings with it the possibility of substituting or exchanging one person for another: the possessor of quantitatively assessed low abilities can, when he fails to fulfill the production goals assigned to him, be replaced by the possessor of greater abilities. In the field of industrial labor, this principle is applied ruthlessly. Top-level sports realizes the principle, for example, in professional team sports, which allow substitutions. Athletes can thus be directly compared to one another on the basis of their market value.

16. The Concept of "Work" in the Language of Sports

The next step of our investigation concerns speech, which, as an instrument of human communication, delivers information concerning the contents of thought and consciousness. Cognitive processes neither arise nor act in isolation but are rather narrowly bound up "with social behavior." They must be seen "in connection with the forms of human social behavior."[1] Speech is defined sociologically as a socially conditioned tool of interpersonal understanding and of systems of thought. Language captures the appearance of the environment and communicates it symbolically. More accurately, social conditions and processes are reflected upon and reprocessed in speech. As the bearer of such facts, speech itself becomes the object of sociological investigation. We shall investigate the concepts which, explicitly or implicitly, refer to the sociological connections between top-level sports and work.

The use of the concept "work" within sports is evident: "Warm-up-work,"* "speed-work," "strength-

* Similar English terms, like "working with weights," are common but less so than in German. [Trans.]

work," "work with balls," "work with the medicine ball," "hurdling work," "weight-work,"[2] "with the quick athletic work of the sprinter," "worked too quickly and too hard," "this work will be sharpened up in the course of the season."[3] The catalogue could easily be extended; it shows the extent to which the terms "work" and "to work" are integral parts of athletic terminology. They allow us to see that the forms of athletic activity can under certain conditions be associated with work. "The fact is that contemporary sports are a hard struggle for achievement and success, a struggle demanding years of hard work."[4]

In understanding top-level sports, the concept of a purposeful system of behavior is important; in it the hallmark of social labor can be seen. If we look more closely at one of the terms from the catalogue mentioned above, we can see that "strength-work" does not evoke the image of an unplanned, goal-less behavior in the consciousness of the athlete or the trainer but rather the image of a planned, purposeful, organized kind of behavior which can be looked upon as a special form of work. Modern physical education's avowed purpose is such that top-level sports and training "is planned, leisure-consuming work targeted for the reaching of a freely chosen goal."[5] With the adoption of the term "work," top-level sports (or rather their theorists) complete the assimilation of a socially defined concept into their own language. Work means a structured kind of activity aimed at an ideal or material goal. To employ the concept "work" means to intend an empirically identical content. This is true for every scientific investigation that analyzes a system of social behavior within the parameters of a specific framework of categorical order. Simply to speak of "work" as a special sort of athletic activity disconfirms the thesis that top-level sports do not display work-like elements of behavior.

The language of sports includes many concepts whose contents are objectively a part of occupational social processes. A concept of this type is "technique": " 'Technique' is a 'basic procedure' which fulfills a certain task. . . . A part of every 'basic procedure' (technique) is the fundamental question, 'What is rational and economical about the sequence of motions of this discipline [of sports]?' The question has nothing to do with individuals but has general validity."[6] "Sports techniques" are therefore to be understood in the sense of rational, generally valid procedures to reach certain goals. Accordingly, one refers to the various movement-techniques of high-jumping as "straddle technique" or "flop-technique."[7] The sociological context is obvious: *Homo ludens* [man the player] remains *Homo faber* [man the maker], even in top-level sports.

17. *Summary*

1. The achievement-principle of the bureaucratically organized sphere of industrial work has been imitated in top-level sports. In the quest for records, in the forms of competition and specialization, in the interaction between athletic and social prestige, in sports-based social mobility, we have proofs of the sociological connection between top-level sports and work. Quite apart from considerations of class or of social status, the ability to achieve can become a constituent element of individual social status in both sectors of behavior. Differing economic and material preconditions are not the point. Simultaneously, a system of behavior which is based on achievement coerces its members into conformity to the existing framework of social behavior.

2. The integrating sociological relationships between top-level sports and work can be discovered in the adoption of the principles of rationalization and in their utilization in analytic training methods, in repetitive athletic activity, in temporal and spatial planning, in bureaucratic measures, in social roles, in specific forms of social cooperation, of technical-rational conceptualization and structuring, and in the attempt to make the rules for athletic behavior

scientific. Top-level sports cannot avoid taking on the characteristics of the division of labor. Nonetheless, there exists for the individual athlete (in contrast to the worker) the possibility of some degree of independence in his behavior and in the exercise of his skills.

3. Like any other form of social labor, individual athletic ability can become objectified into an abstract, quantified commodity. As such, it is separable from the person who produced it and exchangeable in a special market.

4. The jargon of sports makes explicit use of the term "work" as well as other terms drawn from work; in doing so, it refers to the formal and material connections between top-level sports and work.

Our preliminary thesis is, therefore, that top-level sports (but not sports in general) integrates work-like schemes of behavior and intellectual content into its behavioral system. Top-level sports function as a sector of social conformity to industrial, bureaucratic social relationships.

On the basis of the results thus far, we can now call into question some of the current hypotheses about the sociological relationships between sports and work:

1. Sports and work are said to be contrarily structured systems of behavior. This thesis is not tenable as a generalization and must be limited to athletic behavior which is not achievement-oriented. It possesses no validity for the field of top-level sports. A critical differentiation of the concept of sports is absolutely necessary, since scientific research as well

as popular consciousness subsume all sorts of phenomena under the category of sports if they have
some sports-like attributes.

2. Sports and work are said to be similarly structured systems of behavior. Here we can turn around
the arguments made above: the concept of sports is
used without differentiation and needs to be limited
to athletic behavior with a stress on achievement.
This hypothesis is only partly valid, for it concerns
only the field of top-level sports. Still, the hypothesis
says something important about the relationship between sports and work which can be related to the
entire area of sports seen as a sociologically dominant kind of behavior. Every assertion about the phenomenon of top-level sports is relevant for sports in
general, for top-level sports today are the driving
force of the whole system of sports. The first of these
two working hypotheses disguises the objective relationships. An inaccurate and distorted understanding of sports is the inevitable result of [accepting the
first rather than the second hypothesis].

Part II

Sports and Ideology

18. *Notes on the Concept of Ideology*

In his "theory of idols," Francis Bacon described the negative effects of imprecise conceptualization upon human consciousness and thought. Erroneous concepts or "idols" (*idola*) clouded the human spirit so much that "truth was scarcely able to break through to it."[1] Ideologies result from a false consciousness of existing social realities.[2] Thought and reality no longer fit and are held apart from each other by the symbols of ideologized speech. Prejudices, empty formulations, and false concepts arise which distort empirical reality and sanction the forms of social thought. Speech offers men a "pre-structured orientation toward life in the form of a world view that is also a value view; speech, with suggestive and well-nigh inescapable force, thrusts upon men certain forms of imagining, thinking, and behaving."[3] In order to uncover and expose such falsifications of the objective world, one needs critical observation of "socially conditioned deviations from the truth"; one must analyze these deviations and attempt to eliminate them.[4] Are these qualities of conceptualization valid only, when all is said and done, "within the world of human relations"? Is speech functionally adequate to the transmission of empirical reality? Does speech not remain "metaphoric and anthropomorphic"?[5]

19. *Ideological Elements in the Discussion of the Relationship between Sports and Work*

In the discussion of the relationship between sports and work which has taken place in recent years, a typical way of imagining things has emerged: The forms of athletic activity are said to be separate from those of purposeful work behavior because of their goal-free play character. Carl Diem has become prominent as representative of this ideology: sports are "an emergence out of the great realm of life which is play." Play, however, is "purposeless activity for its own sake" and occurs, accordingly, "in contrast to work." Diem attempts to base his assertion upon etymology and translates the word "sport" with the concepts "to amuse oneself" and "to enjoy oneself."[1] But play, in the form of a modern team sport, can no longer be defined as a purposeless system of behavior. Concrete achievement-oriented and prestige-oriented goals are of central significance, e.g., rising (in the sense of social mobility) to a higher level of achievement (league) or attaining economic goals (professional sports, top-level amateur sports). Sports do not occur in the industrial society for irrational motives or for no reason at all but rather with precisely defined intentions, for example: to learn motor skills, for reasons of physical education, for biologic-hygienic considerations of health, to realize sociopolitical goals. By subsuming these kinds of behavior under a socially legitimate institution like top-level sports or physical education in the schools, the behavior can be controlled and determined and kept in a framework.

Many other authors have argued that sports are exempt from the conditions of society. Josef Schmitz sees the following common factors between sports and work: "insuring one's presence in the world or as a person" (creation of wholeness), "a sense of pleasure" (the desire to work or to move about), and service (to oneself or to the society). Neither work nor sports has in his view a dominant significance. The conception of the priority of work is rooted rather in a materialistic world view: "According to materialism, only work is purposeful." In this view, argues Schmitz, man is degraded into a number, "a fixed link in a chain, [a] part in the social machinery. The specifically human no longer plays a role."[2] Sports, Schmitz believes, are pure play and make possible a special ability. He does, however, discuss training methods with the remark that work-like repetitions in order to refine some skill do not lead to the playful mastery of the skill. What Schmitz overlooks is the fact that "playful" is here used to mean "habitual" and that work arrangements can also be "playfully" mastered without on that account losing their characteristics as work. Schmitz attempts with this thesis to obscure the conformity of athletic and working skills and activities so that it seems as if every individual were free to decide if he wishes to do sports as pleasurable satisfaction or as the fulfillment of a duty. One must answer Schmitz: whoever is caught up in the toils of top-level athletic training can scarcely change the work-like structures of such a behavioral system merely by deciding to.

Similarly, M. Zeuner rejects every connection between sports and work which, in his view, Marxist authors have mistakenly asserted. These connections are allegedly incompatible with the "essence" of sports. For Zeuner, sports are the polar opposite to the "world of work." Both realms are to be ranked as "of equal value," but neither one can be derived from the other. "In physical exercise, the emotional strength of mankind manifests itself as the polar opposite of increasingly mechanized work. The polarity is none other than that between life and spirit."[4] But "emotional strength" can also be realized in the various forms of work. The contrast between sports and work can scarcely be demonstrated on the basis of this kind of argument. The same holds true for Zeuner's attempt to distinguish athletic from working behavior: "If hard necessity stands behind one's behavior, the need to master one's essence, a rousing 'Thou must!', then we are dealing with work. If our actions are characterized by free choice, borne by a joyful 'I want to!', then we are dealing with play or physical exercise."[5] But these characteristics are interchangeable. The elements Zeuner describes—free choice (play), coercion (work) or duty (physical exercise)—prove rather that play, sports, and work are part of the same pattern of behavior despite the differing accents. Coercive mechanisms appear, with subtle shades of difference, in all three cases.

Again and again it is asserted that sports and work are similar in motor activity but different in goals: "The motions of work are determined by the goal of production, which lies beyond the human body, but the motions of physical exercise are of the body and are concerned with achievements and experiences of the body in motion."[6] But the varieties of athletic behavior are not only "of the body" but also, in the case of achievement orientation, "of goals set up outside the human body." Athletic skills, as we have shown, can be objectified into exchange commodities. On the other hand, work as a means of material reproduction is also "of the body itself." Like Zeuner, Rumpf tries to "balance" the alleged contrasts between sports and work. He thinks it evident that "handicraft labor and physical exercise achieve a synthesis in the area of physical exercises. Concerned for the all-round education of the body, physical education dare not restrict itself to physical exercises in the narrow sense but must take into account all aspects of bodily being which can serve the educational process."[7] Under the smokescreen of pompous pedagogical terminology, the truth about the achievement-oriented sector of sports is disguised—namely, the adoption of norms and patterns of behavior derived from the occupational areas of social life.

The connection between sports and work is generally and fiercely denied by the official theory of sports. "Ignoring the possibility that human motion can be purposeful and objective (work) and goal-less and subjective (physical exercises), one would violate the essence of physical exercise by classifying it in relation to work." The concept "work" is awkwardly avoided and other terms are substituted for it. Instead of "readiness to work" one speaks of "readiness to exercise," etc.[8] One exception is tolerated during physical-education classes; there it is proper to speak of the way "the individual accomplishes his work and plans and orders the work process. The method of instruction aims at the purposeful and appropriate mastery of the work and demonstrates the dependence of the method upon individual ways of working and of planning the work."[9] But what is here ignored is that sports are a subsystem of the behavioral system of the whole society and, as such, cannot be isolated from the society.

20. *The Ideology of Achievement*

As has been demonstrated, top-level sports have adopted the achievement principle of industrial society. Originally, the achievement principle was connected functionally to the legitimate claim made by sports to further the organic health of the human body; but sports have not remained true to this goal. The contemporary consumer society produces more than is necessary to ensure its existence. Similarly, top-level sports, with their focus on records, no longer serve the purpose of maintaining or improving physical well-being. It is undeniable that the top-level athlete risks physical and psychological injuries which not infrequently leave him an invalid. Indeed, as statistics show, in some cases injuries have led to death. Athletic achievement loses its function and it is transformed into an abstract value sought after even at the cost of extraordinary physical pain.[1] "Achievement has become the absolute yardstick."[2] More accurately expressed, achievement has become an ideology; achievement has become central. The name of the person who has set the record is not important; the quantitatively measurable value is.

What social relevance can such an over-valuation of achievement have?

1. A sociological interpretation might go like this: men strive to realize those values which are topmost in the social scale, assuring themselves thereby high social status and prestige.

2. Psychologists associate an optimal sense of pleasure and a simultaneous optimal satisfaction of drives with every human achievement.

3. Anthropological research perceives a basic pattern of behavior in the permanent quest for higher achievements, behavior which is aimed at the progressive conquest of the environment.

The question is, to what degree are these motivations ideologically exploitable? to what degree do they bring repression with them? That repression is indeed involved can be seen in the continuous development of training and teaching methods and in the bureaucratization of the forms of athletic activity. Planning, repetition, and rational organization determine top-level sports today. On the one hand, propaganda holds that sports offer the possibility of unregulated structures of behavior. On the other hand, sports create a normatively structured field of behavior. This discrepancy can be bridged only by a critical, non-ideological understanding of sports.

21. *Social Functions of the Ideologizing of the Work-Like Structures of Sports*

Ideologies fulfill specific social functions. For one thing, they serve to justify and thus to cement existing social relationships. For another, they have the task of masking objective social relationships. Ideologies have material causes: they serve specific group interests.[1]

One of the most important functions of the ideologies of sports seems to consist of the covering up of the work-like structures of sports. This is done consciously, so that the actual interests of groups can be hidden behind imaginary ideals. Sports become a metaphysically transfigured "mode of being." In sports, the body allegedly reaches its perfection: "Body, soul, and spirit are inseparably bound together: 'mens sana in corpore sano' [a sound mind in a sound body] . . . [The sound body] creates the precondition for a sound spirit."[2] This unproven slogan has long served as an ideological vehicle for physical educators influenced by the humanistic model of education. "The affirmation of sports and thus the affirmation of the body as well as the spirit is a task of modern society that can scarcely be overestimated and which is necessary for maintaining the health of the nation and for combating the harmful effects of civilized life."[3] Hardly anyone now doubts the objective basis of this thesis, but it should not be thoughtlessly made into an argument about the sociobiological function of sports. Its ideological content is all too obvious. It invites misuse.

Friedrich Ludwig Jahn* and his followers conceived of the gymnastics movement as a preliminary field of behavior. Such elements as group discipline, strict rules for motor behavior during the various gymnastic exercises[4], and static physical training (similar to that of military training), made Jahn's gymnastics into an instrument of repressive education making no secret of its hopes for the future. In the shadow of an unconsciously conformist, conservative ideology, which called for traditionalism and subjection to a hierarchically structured social order, the bourgeoisie developed a system of physical hardening for military purposes. The power of the state made good use of this consciousness and its institutional apparatus. Once the state recognized the manifold possibilities for the political exploitation of sports, it invested heavily in an economic sense as well. The sports movement received an institutional basis (sports as a part of physical education in school, colleges of sports education, institutes within universities).

* "Father" Jahn, a Romantic nationalist, began the gymnastics movement in the early nineteenth century. [Trans.]

In the Third Reich, the politicization of sports was perfected, if only in the self-image of the sports movement itself, which was in fact politically broken and reshaped ideologically. Hitler's "fundamentals of education" and the ideology of the "racist state" came to the forefront: the goal of sports lay in the transmission of military virtues: "sports should . . . harden and teach one to endure hardships."[5] The hardening of the body through sports became the first priority of education. "The entire educational work of the racist state . . . consists not in the mere pumping of students full of knowledge but rather in the breeding of bodies sound as a nut. Then comes the furthering of spiritual skills."[6] Hitler made no bones about admitting the function of sports within his imperialistically directed politics: the "racist state" had the task of hardening the body "in order to serve the purpose of preserving the people which the state protects and represents."[7] Boxing and jiujitsu seemed more important to Hitler than "inadequate rifle training. Give the German nation but six million faultlessly, athletically trained bodies, all burning with fanatical love of their fatherland and educated with the highest aggressive spirit, and the nation-state will, if necessary, make an army out of them in less than two years. . . . The hardening of the body will give the individual the conviction of his superiority and the confidence which comes from eternal consciousness of one's own strength. In addition, athletic skills will be learned, which serve as weapons in defense of the [Nazi] movement."[8] Physical education found its rationale in self-defense; but

German history has taught us something rather different.

Anti-intellectualism was another component in Hitler's ideology of sports. "The racist state must . . . begin with the assumption that a less well scientifically educated but physically sounder man, one with a good steady character, one with a joyful sense of decisiveness and a powerful will and dedication to his people, is more valuable than a spiritually rich weakling."[9] "A decayed body [i.e., one belonging to an intellectual] is not in the least made beautiful by a radiant spirit. The most spiritual of educations cannot be justified if the educated person is at the same time physically decayed and crippled, weak in character, indecisive, and cowardly. . . . When the spirit is healthy, it usually resides in a healthy body."[10] Moreover, the greatest athletic achievements come from "aryan men." The "final goal" of sports is not to "cultivate a crop of record-setters" but to "produce sound, sturdy bodies" and to create a military team that can defend itself."[11] The "treacherous and rootless philosophy of spirit" will be replaced by "the philosophy of strength." "A new age has begun. We call it the age of the cultivation of strength. . . . It was a remarkable misunderstanding when educators thought to imitate the Greeks by leading their pupils to spirit (Logos). We ought not to begin where the Greeks left off but must begin where they began, not with the spirit but with the innate type (Physis) [i.e., with the material basis of life]."[12] Physical strength must be set above spiritual strength. In the background stood the fanatical ideology which was to be served by the creation of the physically "sound body of the people." This ideology appeared in the programmatic anti-Semitism of the Nazis' sports propaganda: as an "enemy of the German people," the Jews were excluded from sports: they wanted allegedly to "weaken the German people with international pacifism" and used the sports movement for that purpose; Jewish students would be "buried by the spirit of the team" during physical education classes; because of anatomical-physiological defects, Jews were incapable of athletic achievements.[14] Finally, Jews were too cowardly and lacked "sufficient courage for athletic contests"; they take part in the competition "only when they are sure in advance that they will win."[15]

Both East and West Germany have preserved two hallmarks of sports in Nazi Germany: (1) Sports training and physical education have continued to be authoritarian. In authoritative textbooks one reads, "The pupil must learn to accept the directions of the teacher without receiving extensive explanations and explications of their meaning. In the first place, a child cannot understand all the explanations and, in the second place, there is frequently too little time for explanations, especially in dangerous situations. Subordination is therefore a necessity."[16]

(2) The consciousness of the person who does or administers sports has remained predominantly unpolitical. This was manifested during the Olympic Games of 1968, in Mexico City. Despite the war in Vietnam, the occupation of Czechoslovakia, and political unrest in Mexico, the games went on. The pol-

itical protest of two black American athletes was both justified and paradigmatic, and they were immediately excluded from the American team. White repression versus black passive resistance exists today even in the sphere of sports, where racial discrimination has allegedly been overcome.

22. *Bourgeois-Romantic Tendencies*

The sphere of behavior in which sports occur may seem at first glance not to be integrated into the world of work, but we have seen that the bureaucratizing of sports brings with it the administrative forms typical of industrial society. This socially determined conformity of patterns of behavior is, however, as we have already indicated, covered up by such overblown, ideologized goals as popular health, "liberal" education, recreation, and "alternative to work." The sociological, genetic connection between sports and work is denied. An example of this sort of development can be found in the German Gymnastics League (*Deutscher Turner-Bund*—DTB), the oldest organized conservative sports organization in Germany.* What Friedrich Ludwig Jahn had proclaimed a half century earlier was to have achieved unlimited validity in a changed historical, social situation: "The art of gymnastics will restore the rule of equality in human education which has been lost; it will subordinate one-sided spiritualization to true

* Rigauer refers to the DTB, originally founded in the nineteenth century as the German Gymnastics Association (*Deutsche Turnerschaft*) as if it were a contemporary organization. [Trans.]

physicality; it will encourage a newly regained masculinity as a necessary counterbalance to excessive refinement; it will encompass the whole man in youthful community."[1] Jahn's program is "created as if for our time, for a technical age, with its intensified intellectual exertion and its diminished need for physical effort, demands that man find some kind of bodily compensation. . . . Only that man can be called educated whose being is well-rounded."[2] Gymnastics is "the people's concern": "Work on a broadly public scale is the essence of German gymnastics; the sound struggle for achievement is acknowledged as a means to develop the personality." "Popular physical education must remain the rule!"[3] At the same time, gymnastics is sharply distinguished from sports, for sports are striving for victory in competition, for "absolute records," and for "experience at the limits of achievement" while gymnastics pursues "the end of physical education."[4] But gymnastics has long since accepted the behavioral and intellectual models that we have found to be typical of top-level sports—i.e., rationalizing measures, achievement-orientation, and "technicizing."[5]

Industrial society seems to have a vested interest in an ideologized conception of sports, because such a conception applies bourgeois virtues to the norms of athletic behavior.[6] Many of the codified rules for athletic behavior sound like middle-class commandments: "Set yourself a goal!" Prepare yourself "conscientiously" for your task! Recognize the coach's authority "voluntarily" and "completely"! "Honor" the work of "functionaries and referees"! Be a "modest winner" and a "brave loser"! "The good of the group rather than the good of the individual"![7] Concepts like drive, conscientiousness, recognition of authority and of the achievements of one's superiors, modesty and shyness, the good of the group, etc., encourage conformity to the existing system of action and control. These concepts indicate the work-like structures of sports, for those who would master the work-process with optimal success must strive for their goals, work conscientiously, acknowledge authorities (i.e., the possessors of the means of production or of high social status), assume a certain external modesty, etc. Under the pretext of formally binding rules of sports behavior, what will be demanded of athletes is precisely what will be demanded of them in the world of work. By integrating middle-class virtues within themselves, sports take on—unconsciously—schemes of behavior derived from society in general—schemes marked with regressive consciousness. Sports are no separate realm of activity but an agent of socialization through which the actor is forced to conform to the forms and contents of society's framework of relationships.

Once divested of its social and work-like structures, the concept of sports seems to be colored by Oswald Spengler's dilettantish conception of the "decline of the West." A number of contemporary authors look upon sports as a possible means to avoid the predicted collapse of the West into decadence. It is argued that the athletic person is "a new being" whose stunning physical characteristics and "sober clarity of thought" often appear to intellectuals as primitive qualities. "A new feeling is expressed in form and content. Health, strength, and an inner and outer beauty" are "the unconsciously sought-after goals" [of this new being]. The "foundation" is allegedly ready "upon which a new Western Civilization can grow."[8] Since sports have been declared to be the institution for the salvation and preservation of Western culture, they are naturally ideologized to high degree. The goal of sports no longer follows from a critical understanding of empirical facts but from unrealistic fantasies. The concept of sport loses its objective social basis and becomes the vehicle of ideologies, interest, and traditions. Whatever this concept dictates, practice must accept: interest groups (sports clubs and organizations, the institutions of physical education) and the state attempt to make sports serve their ends.

Conclusion: Toward a New Understanding of Sports

Sports imitate purposeful, rational, work-like behavior patterns. They function as instruments of socialization, with the behavioral and intellectual contents of industrial society. Recreational sports are something else again; the less the form of athletic action is rule-bound and subordinated to the value of achievement, the more likely that action is to *dis*integrate the behavioral patterns of industrial society. As we tried to prove above, the sports movement runs the continual danger of taking on work-like, conformist, and nonpolitical models of thought. Sociologically considered, however, sports do have the capacity to withstand this trend. Sports could develop a new self-conception. The preconditions for such a new self-conception are as follows:

1. The dissolution of work-like structures of behavior. To achieve this goal it is necessary to do away with repressive measures of rationalization and to unmask the fetish of achievement. Doubtless there have been attempts to take this road even in contem-

porary sports practice, for example, the so-called "Second Way" of the German Sports Federation.*

The dissolution of conformist thought and behavior. The freedom of the individual to act can be quantitatively and qualitatively widened by independent choices, not by rules, bureaucratic edicts, guidelines, and obedience. A widening of choice implies the democratization of the whole enterprise of sports; it implies the systematic realization of teamwork and cooperation, for athletic games are an ideal field of experimentation for socializing into democratic patterns of behavior, not only through interactions among players of a single team but also among "opposing" players—as they are falsely named. (Thus is every role socially efficacious and definable through its "counter-role.")

3. Politicizing of sports. Empirical studies demonstrate that athletes have genuine political interests contrary to those of the existing state. Pretending that sports are "apolitical" only disguises this fact.

4. The de-ideologizing of the sports movement. If there is to be a new conception of sports that makes them fit for a process of liberal education, this conception must be oriented to an understanding of sports based on empirical reality and on enlightened principles rather than on wishful thinking and illusions.

From these theses it might be possible to derive a modern sports program whose contents could be

---

* The German Sports Federation's "Second Way," begun in 1964, seeks to increase public participation in noncompetitive physical activity. [Trans.]

drawn from an awareness of the contradictions of sports as they are today. A point of departure would be the critical illumination of the connections between sports and society. The results of such an analysis could be condensed into undogmatic "guidelines" and put into practice. The bureaucratic organs of the sports movement must be more efficiently controlled by the memberships. Sports must dedicate themselves more intensively than they have to social and educational tasks, must free themselves financially and ideologically from state control, and must make the satisfaction of individual needs the central purpose of doing sports. Sports will arrive at the stage of critical self-awareness when they are perceived as part of society. The changes necessary for sports must be part of changes in society.

Afterword

Scarcely anyone today doubts that there are social and historical interactions between sports and work. Indeed, they are more pronounced than ever, in the training technology and rationalized forms of organization in top-level "amateur" and professional sports, and in the maintenance of physical fitness (i.e., labor power) in recreational sport, which turns out to be a miniature verson of top-level sports. To this extent, my 1969 analysis seems as timely as ever. The basic argument has maintained its provisional validity, because social relationships its provisional validity because social relationships in the East and the West alike have in recent years which play and work might form a life-enhancing unity. Quite the contrary. In light of events, a second edition of *Sport und Arbeit* is completely justified.

This present Afterword does not provide me with space adequate to a thorough treatment of the many questions and criticisms occasioned by *Sport und Arbeit*. I want, nonetheless, briefly to respond to a few of the central points that have been raised.

A frequent objection is that my analysis is not "empirical." If one conceives of social-scientific empiricism in a narrow and dogmatic fashion, then the objection is valid: the analysis derives neither from "representative" questionnaires nor from "standardized" observations. Instead, I've based my discussion upon a kind of empiricism which contemporary social-scientific practice scorns and derides—that is, upon my own subjective experiences in top-level sports and in industrial work. And I have dared to use these experiences scientifically. Unfortunately, I failed to make my background clear to the reader, and that has been held against me. *Sport und Arbeit* ought, accordingly, to be understood as my own sociologically informed practical experience. In these experiences there is an empirical content, just as there is in the generally recognized empirical sources whose data I draw upon in order to develop and substantiate my theses. In other words, I have used subjective experiences in an attempt to show that sports demonstrate the same structural characteristics as work in an industrial-capitalist society. I have sought to illuminate the social instrumentalities which make sports possible. In doing this I must confess that I have utilized a conception of work which is not precise enough for the kind of comparative analysis of sports which I have undertaken; this has been pointed out to me by a number of critics, among them Hans Lenk and Sven Güldenpfennig. The concept of work I have used remains too general, not to say too formal and, in a certain sense, ahistorical. I see now that it is insufficient in a sociological analysis of sports and work to limit the discussion to abstract social relationships. One must also recognize that we are dealing with a specific

historically determined kind of work—that of industrial capitalism with all its life-disturbing effects.
Since this "bad" model of work acts upon all aspects
of social life, sports too are affected. Sports too are
in danger of becoming a life-disturbing model of
human behavior. This in increasingly evident in top-
level sports. In a provisional way I have already
touched upon the interrelationships between sports
and industrial-capitalist work in my section on "The
Commodity Character of Top-Level Sports." The insights obtained in that section have led me to a further analysis of the problem sketched out above (see
my *The Structure of Commodities and the Conditions of Top-Level Sports* [1979]). I derive my discussion from the paradigm of capitalistic commodity
production and consumption which, because of its
ability to dominate the system's socializing functions, establishes interpersonal relationships. The
result is that commodity relationships and the pattern of economic exchanges appear even outside the
sphere of economic activity per se. Within the framework of these categories, sports too are conceived of
as a type of behavior determined by material and
ideal "surplus value," exchange relationships, and
objectification.* Therein lies the danger of the creation of an alienated consciousness, alienated in the
sense that doing sport and watching sport both lead
to modes of behavior which have less to do with the

* "Surplus value" (*Mehrwert*) is a Marxist term referring to the value of
labor above and beyond what is necessary for the laborer and his family
to survive; this "surplus value" is appropriated by the capitalist. "Objectification" (*Vergegenständlichung*) refers to the transformation of a
person or a process into a thing, an object. [Trans.]

unfolding of individual needs and capacities than with adaptation to externally imposed, quantified, comparable modes of behavior which are based upon formalized socially determined techniques.

Let us return to our point of departure. There would be no problem about limiting the contents of *Sport und Arbeit* if we had already achieved the utopian possibility of social labor that is completely free of external control. Lacking this kind of possibility as a historical prerequisite, my commentary about a "new understanding of sports" remained abstract and unsatisfying. As already shown, an imprecise conception of social labor, without the above-mentioned sketch of a more humane model of work, led necessarily to a negative judgment concerning the relations between sports and work. The alternative to the present system cannot be "dissolution of work-like structures of behavior in sports" but rather the unity of sports and work under social conditions of autonomy and self-determination.

Since space is short, let me gather together in systematic form the criticisms leveled against *Sport und Arbeit*:

1. Criticism of the underlying concept of work and its comparative-analytic application to the realm of sports;

2. Criticism of my neglect of other social (also historical) and anthropological (also psychological and biological) aspects of sports behavior and activity;

3. Criticism of the inadequate "empirical" proof of my theses;

4. Criticism of the absence of practical consequences of my analysis;

5. Charges that the "New Left" wants to throttle and destroy sports.

I have already responded to the first and third points. The second point includes the problem of individuation and socialization, upon which I am currently working. As to the fourth point, I should remark that I did not intend my book as a guide to actions the pedagogical basis for which were lacking at that time. The fifth point reveals an emotional criticism which derives from the political background of sports. Even today criticism of sports remains unpopular in the mass media and in the clubs and associations which continue to promote uncritical conceptions of the contents of sports and of the questions that might be raised about sports behavior.

In writing *Sport und Arbeit* I undertook the development of a theory in which sport is not denigrated either as social institution nor as subjective activity. Let me interject the slogan that sports cannot be "better" than their social context and circumstances. I intended merely to call into question certain developments and thereby to challenge the reader to critical reflection aiming at emancipatory change and progress in sports.

Friedrichsfehn
August 1979

Notes

Translator's Introduction

1. *Homo Ludens* (London: Temple Smith, 1970), p. 19.
2. *Sports and Pastimes of the People of England*, 2nd ed. (London: Thomas Tegg, 1838), pp. xvii–xviii.
3. *Soziologie des Sports* (Berlin: Verlag von August Reher, 1921), p. 25.
4. *Ibid.*, p. 77.
5. Wohl's most important work is *Die gesellschaftlich-historischen Grundlagen des bürgerlichen Sports* (Cologne: Pahl-Rugenstein, 1973). He has also published numerous essays in *The International Review of Sport Sociology* and in *Sportwissenschaft*. On Wohl's work, see John M. Hoberman, "Communist Sport Theory Today: The Case of Andrzej Wohl," *Arena Review*, 4, no. 1 (February 1980): 13–16.
6. For a summary of the Marxist view of sports, see my *From Ritual to Record: The Nature of Modern Sports* (New York: Columbia University Press, 1978), pp. 57–64.
7. Ulrike Prokop, *Soziologie der Olympischen Spiele* (Munich: Carl Hanser, 1971), p. 21.
8. *Sport and Work*, p. 27.
9. *Ibid.*, p. 57–58.
10. *Ibid.* p. 44.
11. *Ibid.* p. 47.
12. *Ibid.* p. 68.
13. *Ibid.*, p. 71.
14. *Ibid.*, p. 76.
15. *Ibid.*, p. 78.
16. *Ibid.*, p. 79.
17. *Ibid.*, p. 85.
18. *Ibid.*, p. 92.
19. *Ibid.*, p. 100.

20. Among the most important works are Gerhard Vinnai, *Fußballsport als Ideologie* (Frankfurt: Europäische Verlagsanstalt, 1970); Prokop, *Soziologie der Olympischen Spiele*; Jac-Olaf Böhme, Jürgen Gadow, Sven Güldenpfennig, Jörn Jensen, and Renate Pfister, *Sport im Spätkapitalismus* (Frankfurt: Limpert, 1971); Karin Rittner, *Sport und Arbeitsteilung* (Frankfurt: Limpert, 1976); Ginette Berthaud, Jean-Marie Brohm, François Gantheret, and Pierre Laguillaumie, *Sport, culture et répression* (Paris: François Maspero, 1972); Jean-Marie Brohm, *Critiques du sport* (Paris: Christian Bourgeois, 1976); Paul Hoch, *Rip Off the Big Game* (New York: Anchor Books, 1972).

21. Böhme et al., *Sport im Spätkapitalismus*, p. 37.

22. Vinnai, *Fußballsport als Ideologie*, p. 65.

23. A. Krovoza and T. Leithäuser, Preface to *ibid.*, p. 8.

24. See Hans Lenk, "'Manipulation' oder 'Emanzipation' im Leistungssport?" *Sportwissenschaft*, 3, no. 1 (1973): 9–40; Hans Lenk, *Leistungssport: Ideologie oder Mythos?* (Stuttgart: Kohlhammer, 1972); Josef N. Schmitz, *Sport und Leibeserziehung zwischen Spätkapitalismus und Frühsozialismus* (Schorndorf: Karl Hofmann, 1974); Ommo Grupe, "Produkt der Gesellschaft?" *Die Politische Meinung*, 17, no. 143 (1972): 36–43; Ommo Grupe, "Leistung und Leistungsprinzip im Sport," *Sinn und Unsinn des Leistungsprinzips*, ed. Max Müller (Munich: DTV, 1974), pp. 111–38; and my own *From Ritual to Record*, pp. 69–89.

25. See Paul Kunath, "Persönlichkeitsentwicklung und Sport," *Theorie und Praxis der Körperkultur*, 17 (1968): 596; Fred Gras, "About the Way of Life and Development of Personality of Competitive Sportsmen," *International Review of Sport Sociology*, 11, no. 1 (1976): 77–81; Andrzej Wohl, "Competitive Sport and Its Social Function," *International Review of Sport Sociology*, 5 (1970): 117–24.

26. See Michel Bouet, *Les Motivations des sportifs* (Paris: Editions universitaires, 1969); Hartmut Gabler, *Leistungsmotivation im Hochleistungssport* (Schorndorf: Karl Hofmann, 1972); Paul Weiss, *Sport* (Carbondale: Southern Illinois University Press, 1969); Howard S. Slusher, *Man, Sport and Existence* (Philadelphia: Lea & Febiger, 1967); Harold A. VanderZwaag, *Toward a Philosophy of Sport* (Reading, Massachusetts: Addison-Wesley, 1972).

27. Ulrich Dix, *Sport und Sexualität* (Frankfurt: März Verlag, 1972), p. 59.

28. See Lenk, "'Manipulation' oder Emanzipation' im Leistungssport?"

29. Vinnai, *Fußballsport als Ideologie*, p. 65.

30. For a discussion of this topic, including references to the literature, see my *From Ritual to Record*, pp. 130–36.

31. In addition to the seventeen items cited in my *From Ritual to Record* (p. 174), see Benjamin Lowe, Peter Hill, and Jean Roberts, "A Cross-Cultural Study of Athletes Representing Four Countries in the Commonwealth Games," *Australian Journal of Health, Physical Education and Recreation*, 70 (December 1975): 22–26; Richard E. and Maureen R. DuWors, "Reasons for Participation in Male Amateur Sport and Education Status of the Father . . . ," *Sociology of Sport/Sociologie du sport*, ed. Fernand Landry and William A. R. Orban (Miami and Québec: Symposia Specialists/Editeur officiel, 1978), pp. 67–78; A. M. Maksimenko and Antoine Barushimana, "Attitude Towards Sport Activity of Top-Class Athletes of Central Africa," *International Review of Sport Sociology*, 13, no. 2 (1978): 37–50.

32. Taken from Günther Lüschen, "Soziale Schichtung und Soziale Mobilität bei jungen Sportlern," *Kölner Zeitschrift für Soziologie und Sozialpsychologie*, 15 (1963): 74–93.

33. Taken from Klaus Prenner, "Leistungsmotivation im Spitzensport," *Leibeserziehung*, 20, no. 11 (November 1971): 370–73.

34. *Sport and Work*, p. 2.

Introduction

1. The beginnings of contemporary sport lie in mid-nineteenth-century England, simultaneous with the beginning of industrialization. For enlightening comments on this matter, see A. Wohl, "Die gesellschaftlich-historischen Grundlagen des bürgerlichen Sports," *Wissenschaftliche Zeitschriften d. DHfK*, 6 (1964): 5–93.

2. Jürgen Habermas represents this thesis in his essay, "Soziologische Notizen zum Verhältnis von Arbeit und Freizeit," in *Konkrete Vernunft. Festschrift für E. Rothacker* (Bonn, 1958), pp. 219–31. He speaks of "suspensive" leisure-time behavior, by

which he means the extension of work-like behavior into leisure time.

3. H. Linde, *Zur Soziologie des Sports. Versuch einer empirischen Kritik soziologischer Theoreme*, in *Sport und Leibeserziehung*, ed. Helmuth Plessner et al. (Munich, 1967), pp. 103–20.

4. *Ibid.*, p. 119.

5. K. Popper, *Logik der Sozialwissenschaften*, in *Kölner Zeitschrift Für Soziologie und Sozialpsychologie*, 16 (1962): 235.

1. Two Contrasting Interpretations of the Sports-Work Problem

1. C. Diem, *Wesen und Lehre des Sports und der Leibeserziehung* (Berlin, 1960), p. 3.

2. *Ibid.*, pp. 25–26.

3. C. Diem, *Spätlese am Rhein* (Frankfurt, 1957), pp. 6–7.

4. E. Schildge and W. Gerschler, *Psychologische Probleme des Leistungssports*, in *Jahrbuch des Sports* 1965/1966, p. 30.

5. W. Daume, "Freiheit und Verantwortung im Sport," in *Der Wetteifer*, 2. Kongress f. Leibeserziehung 5.-8. 10. 61 in Göttingen (Frankfurt & Vienna, 1962), p. 173.

6. A. Gehlen, "Sport und Gesellschaft," in *Das große Spiel* (Frankfurt-Hamburg, 1965), p. 28.

7. M. Horkheimer and Theodor Adorno, *Dialektik der Aufklärung* (Amsterdam, 1947), p. 51.

8. Habermas, "Soziologische Notizen," p. 227.

9. F. G. Jünger, *Die Spiele. Ein Schlüssel zu ihrer Bedeutung* (Frankfurt, 1953), p. 216.

10. H. Plessner, "Die Funktion des Sports in der industriellen Gesellschaft," in *Leibeserziehung und Sport in der modernen Gesellschaft* (Weinheim, 1966), p. 26.

11. Christian Graf Von Krockow, "Die Bedeutung des Sports für die moderne Gesellschaft," in *Jahrbuch des Sports* 1957–1958 (Frankfurt, 1958), p. 29.

12. G. v. Mengden, "Grundsätzliches zum Problem der Freizeit," in *Jahrbuch des Sports* 1957–1958 (Frankfurt, 1958), p. 18ff.

13. K. Meinel, *Bewegungslehre* (Berlin, 1966), p. 24.

14. G. Erbach, "Sportwissenschaft und Sportsoziologie," *Wissenschaftliche Zeitschrift der DHfK*, 7 (1965): 35n.

15. A. Wohl, "Theorie der Körperkultur als gesellschaft-swissenschaftliches und naturwissenschaftliches Problem," *Theorie und Praxis der Körperkultur*, 5 (1956), p. 500.

16. K. Meinel, *Bewegungslehre*, p. 27.

17. A. Wohl, *Die gesellschaftlich-historischen Grundlagen der bürgerlichen Sports*, in *Wissenschaftliche Zeitschrift der DHfK*, 6 (1964): 52.

18. Vide M. Zeuner, "Murti Bing und das Verhältnis von Leibesübung und Arbeit," *Leibesübungen*, 11 (June 1960): 13–16.

2. The Necessity of Social Labor

1. A. Gehlen, "Ein Bild vom Menschen," in *Anthropologische Forschung* (Hamburg, 1964), pp. 46ff.

2. H. Marcuse, "Über die philosophischen Grundlagen des wirtschafts-wissenschaftlichen Arbeitsbegriffs," *Kultur und Gesellschaft*, 2 (Frankfurt, 1965), p. 21.

3. *Ibid.*, pp. 13ff.

4. *Ibid.*, p. 45.

5. O. Lipmann, *Lehrbuch der Arbeitswissenschaft* (Jena, 1932), p. 3.

3. The Achievement Principle in Sports and Work

1. T. Parsons, *Beiträge zur soziologischen Theorie* (Neuwied & Berlin, 1964), p. 241.

2. *Ibid.*, p. 200.

3. *Ibid.*, p. 149.

4. Top-Level Sports

1. Psychoanalytic theory offers an explanation for this: the emotional attachment of an individual to an idealized object is transformed into hatred at the moment of disillusionment.

2. G. Lüschen, "Der Leistungssport in seiner Abhängigkeit vom soziokulturellen System," *Zentralblatt für Arbeitswissenschaft*, 19 (1962): 187.

3. H. Lenk, *Werte—Ziele—Wirklichkeit der modernen Olympischen Spiele* (Schorndorf, 1964), p. 84.

4. C. Diem, *Wesen und Lehre des Sports und der Leibeserziehung* (Berlin, 1960), pp. 13–14.

5. Sport psychologists have tried to define athletic achievement as a psychological experience—the individual experiences situations of special quality during the achieving. These psychologists ignore the social determinants of the situation.

6. W. Sieger, "Produktionskraft, Mensch und Körperkultur," *Wissenschaftliche Zeitschrift der DHfK*, 6 (1964): 43.

7. *Ibid.*, pp. 51ff.

8. B. Jonas, "Die sportliche Leistung in den Wertvorstellungen der Jugend," *Die Leistung* (Schorndorf, 1964), pp. 182–91.

5. "Achievement"

1. K. Deschka, *Trainingslehre und Organisationslehre des Sports* (Vienna & Munich, 1961), pp. 6–7.

2. F. W. Taylor, *Die Grundsätze wissenschaftlicher Betriebsführung* (Munich & Berlin, 1913), p. 7.

3. *Ibid.*, p. 11.

4. A. Wohl, *Gesellschaftlich-historische Grundlagen*, p. 52.

5. W. Umminger, *Helden—Götter—Übermenschen. Eine Kulturgeschichte menschlicher Höchstleistungen* (Düsseldorf & Vienna, 1962), p. 367.

6. T. Nett, *Modernes Training weltbester Mittel- und Langstreckler* (Berlin & Munich, 1966), p. 11.

7. K. Deschka, *Trainingslehre*, p. 6.

8. Theodor W. Adorno, *Prismen, Kulturkritik und Gesellschaft* (Frankfurt, 1955), p. 75.

9. A. Wohl, *Gesellschaftlich-historische Grundlagen*, p. 22.

10. G. Lüschen, "Der Leistungssport," p. 186.

11. Chr. Graf v. Krockow, "Der Wetteifer in der industriellen Gesellschaft und im Sport," *Der Wetteifer* (Frankfurt & Vienna, 1962), p. 59.

12. T. Parsons, *Beiträge zur soziologischen Theorie*, p. 180.

13. H. Lenk, *Werte-Ziele-Wirklichkeit*, p. 84.

6. On the Parallel Rationalization of Athletic and Occupational Behavior

1. M. Weber, *Wirtschaft und Gesellschaft* (Cologne & Berlin, 1964), 1: 22.

2. O. Lipmann, *Lehrbuch der Arbeitswissenschaft*, p. 160.

3. *Ibid.*, pp. 161–62.

7. Complex Methods of Work and Training

    1. J. Habermas, "Soziologische Notizen," p. 221.

    2. H. Lenk, *Werte-Ziele-Wirklichkeit*, p. 79.

8. Analytical Methods of Work and Training: Loads

    1. T. Nett, *Modernes Training*, p. 13. (Note that the use of the term "work" in this context refers to the degree to which athletic training is now understood as a kind of work.)

    2. W. Gerschler, "Langstreckenlauf," in *Der Lauf*, Internationale Arbeitstagung. Ed. Deutscher-Leichtathletik-Verband (1958), p. 108.

    3. The other two examples are to be interpreted the same way.

    4. F. W. Taylor, *Grundsätze*, p. 40.

    5. J. Habermas, "Soziologische Notizen," p. 221.

    6. *Ibid.*, p. 227.

    7. F. W. Taylor, *Grundsätze*, p. 12.

    8. H. Hilf, *Arbeitswissenschaft* (Munich, 1967), p. 190.

    9. T. Nett and J. Jonath, *Kraftübungen zur Konditionsarbeit* (Berlin-Charlottenburg, 1960), p. 77.

    10. Everett S. Dean, *Progressive Basketball* (Palo Alto, 1947), p. 158. (*G, G', F, C* represent playing positions.)

    11. T. Nett, *Modernes Training*, p. 88.

    12. G. Friedmann, *Zukunft der Arbeit* (Cologne, 1953), p. 203.

    13. Th. W. Adorno, *Prismen*, p. 76.

    14. G. Friedmann, *Grenzen der Arbeitsteilung* (Frankfurt, 1959), p. 77.

    15. H. Popitz et al., *Technik und Industriearbeit* (Tübingen, 1957), p. 157.

    16. J. Habermas, "Soziologische Notizen," p. 227.

    17. G. Friedmann, *Grenzen*, p. 144.

10. Timing and Bureaucratizing

    1. F. W. Taylor, *Grundsätze*, p. 4.

    2. K. Deschka, *Trainingslehre*, p. 178.

    3. *Soziologie*, ed. R. König (Frankfurt & Hamburg, 1960), pp. 46ff.

4. W. Tröger, "Die Organisation des deutschen Sports," *Das Große Spiel* ed. U. Schultz (Frankfurt & Hamburg, 1965), p. 45.
5. R. Mayntz, *Soziologie der Organisation* (Hamburg, 1963), p. 86.
6. F. W. Taylor, *Grundsätze*, p. 67.
7. R. König, ed., *Soziologie*, p. 127.
8. *Ibid.*, pp. 47ff.

11. The Work-Like Role-System of Top-Level Sports

1. *Ibid.*, p. 127.

12. Team-Like and Structure-Like Cooperation

1. H. Popitz, *Technik und Industriearbeit*, p. 34.
2. *Ibid.*, p. 52.
3. *Ibid.*, p. 55.
4. *Ibid.*, p. 61.
5. *Ibid.*, p. 82.
6. G. Friedmann, *Zukunft der Arbeit*, pp. 29ff.
7. *Ibid.*, p. 36.

13. Technical Rationality—a Hallmark of Modern Sports

1. H. Popitz, *Technik und Industriearbeit*, p. 92.
2. M. Horkheimer and Th. Adorno, *Dialektik*, pp. 17ff.
3. *Ibid.*, p. 18.
4. A. Gehlen, "Sport und Gesellschaft," p. 29.
5. *Ibid.*, p. 30.
6. F. G. Jünger, *Die Perfektion der Technik* (Frankfurt, 1953), p. 149.

14. The "Scientification" of Top-Level Sports and Work

1. F. W. Taylor, *Grundsätze*, p. 68.
2. *Ibid.*, p. 24.
3. H. Hilf, *Arbeitswissenschaft*, pp. 49ff.
4. K. Meinel, *Bewegungslehre*, p. 20.
5. F. B. Gilbreth, "Die Wissenschaft des Managements führt zur Arbeitsökonomie," in K. Pentzlin, ed., *Meister der Rationalisierung* (Düsseldorf & Vienna, 1963), p. 240.
6. K. Meinel, *Bewegungslehre*, p. 102.

7. K. Kohl, "Psychologische Aspekte des Leistungssports" *Zentralblatt für Arbeitswissenschaft und Fachberichte aus der sozialen Betriebs-Praxis*, 16 (December 1962): 181.

8. H. Hilf, *Arbeitswissenschaft*, p. 47.

15. Top-Level Sports as a Commodity

1. K. Marx, *Das Kapital* (Berlin, 1961), 1: 39.
2. *Ibid.*, p. 593.
3. *Ibid.*
4. H. Popitz, *Technik und Industriearbeit*, p. 7.
5. G. Friedmann, *Zukunft*, pp. 159ff.

16. The Concept of "Work" in the Language of Sports

1. E. Topitsch, ed., *Logik der Sozialwissenschaft* (Cologne & Berlin, 1966), p. 17.
2. *Internationale Arbeitstagung, "Kondition,"* ed. Deutscher-Leichtathletik-Verband (1958), p. 58.
3. *Ibid., "Der Lauf,"* ed. Deutscher-Leichtathletik-Verband (1958), pp. 79, 81.
4. E. Schildge and W. Gerschler, *Psychologische Probleme*, p. 34.
5. K. Deschka, *Trainingslehre*, p. 6.
6. T. Nett, *Das Übungs-und Trainingsbuch der Leichtathletik* (Berlin, 1956), p. 35.
7. *Ibid.*

18. Notes on the Concept of Ideology

1. F. Bacon, "Die Idolenlehre," in K. Lenk, ed., *Ideologie* (Berlin & Neuwied, 1964), p. 63.
2. Th. W. Adorno, W. Dirks, eds., *Soziologische Exkurse* (Frankfurt, 1956), p. 175.
3. E. Topitsch, *Logik*, p. 33.
4. *Ibid.*, p. 28.
5. H. Barth, *Wahrheit und Ideologie* (Erlenbach-Zürich & Stuttgart, 1961), pp. 219ff.

19. Ideological Elements in the Discussion of the Relationship between Sports and Work

1. C. Diem, *Wesen und Lehre*, p. 2.
2. J. Schmitz, "Arbeit und Leibesübungen im Sinngefüge des Daseins," *Leibesübungen*, 19 (February 1960): 5.
3. *Ibid.*, p. 7.
4. Zeuner, "Murti Bing," p. 15.
5. *Ibid.*
6. E. Rumpf, "Leibesübungen und Arbeit in der Leibeserziehung," *Leibesübungen*, 11 (June 1960): p. 16.
7. *Ibid.*, p. 18.
8. H. Bernett, ed., *Terminologie der Leibeserziehung* (Schorndorf, 1962), pp. 15ff.

20. The Ideology of Achievement

1. The athletes of the industrial nations carried their preparations for the Olympic Games in Mexico City, 1968, to an absurdity: shotputters pushed as much as 100 tons weekly; rowers covered as much as 29 km daily; runners exposed themselves to extremely rarified atmosphere at heights above 2,000 m or ran as much as 750 km a month; a comment by Peter Snell, goldmedalist from 1964, exposes the inhumanity of such training loads: "After training, I wept from exhaustion" (*Der Spiegel*, 22 [October 7, 1968]): 94ff.
2. E. Schildge and W. Gerschler, *Psychologische Probleme*, pp. 29–30.

21. Social Functions of the Ideologizing of the Work-Like Structures of Sports

1. Werner Hofmann, *Universität, Ideologie, Gesellschaft* (Frankfurt, 1968), pp. 49ff.
2. B. Heck, "Die Bedeutung der Leibesübungen für den Staat," *Der Mensch unserer Zeit und die Leibesbungen*, (Frankfurt, 1959), p. 69.
3. J. Nöcker, "Die Stellung des Sports in unserer Gesellschaft," *Sportforum der SPD*, November 10, 1964 (Bad Godesberg, 1964), p. 22.
4. Cf. K. Meinel, *Bewegungslehre*, p. 32.
5. A. Hitler, *Mein Kampf* (Munich, 1943), p. 455.

6. *Ibid.*, p. 452.
7. *Ibid.*, p. 453.
8. *Ibid.*, pp. 611–12.
9. *Ibid.*, p. 452.
10. *Ibid.*, p. 453.
11. H. Bernett, ed., *Nationalsozialistische Leibeserziehung* (Schorndorf, 1966), p. 219.
12. *Ibid.*, p. 56.
13. *Ibid.*, p. 37.
14. *Ibid.*, p. 38.
15. *Ibid.*, p. 40.
16. F. Fetz, *Allgemeine Methodik der Leibesübungen* (Frankfurt & Vienna, 1964), p. 133.

22. Bourgeois-Romantic Tendencies

1. H. Brüggemann, "Jahn und die Gegenwart," *Jahrbuch der Turnkunst*, 58 (1964): 17. (Quotation from Jahn himself.)
2. *Ibid.*
3. *Ibid.*, p. 19.
4. *Ibid.*, p. 18.
5. Simply from historical reasons, gymnastics must be given a special place in the history of German sports because it helped to found the German sports movement.
6. This is as true for the so-called late-capitalist bourgeois society as well as for the so-called socialist society [of the Communist bloc].
7. K. Deschka, *Trainingslehre*, p. 266.
8. H. Altrock, *Die kulturellen Aufgaben des deutschen Sports* (Krevelaer, 1949), pp. 23–24.

Index